DAMIEN
The Making of a Saint

Mutual Publishing

Copyright © 2011 by Mutual Publishing

No part of this book may be reproduced in any form or by any electronic or mechanical means, including information storage and retrieval devices or systems, without prior written permission from the publisher, except that brief passages may be quoted for reviews.

All rights reserved

ISBN-10: 1-56647-946-0
ISBN-13: 978-1-56647-946-2
Library of Congress Control Number: 2011926149

First Printing, August 2011

Mutual Publishing, LLC
1215 Center Street, Suite 210
Honolulu, Hawai'i 96816
Ph: (808) 732-1709
Fax: (808) 734-4094
e-mail: info@mutualpublishing.com
www.mutualpublishing.com

Printed in Korea

Acknowledgments

Many hearts and minds helped to make this book possible. Prime among them: In Louvain, Belgium, Father Paul Macken, retired archivist for the Sacred Hearts Fathers. In Syracuse, New York, Sister Mary Laurence Hanley, director and historian of the Cause of Blessed Marianne Cope. In Hawai'i, Father Chris Keahi, Provincial Superior for the Fathers of the Sacred Hearts. Patrick Downes, editor of the *Hawaii Catholic Herald*. Frank Bridgewater, editor of the *Honolulu Star-Advertiser*. Patrick Boland, lifelong friend of Kalaupapa. Kawika Eyre, Lawrence Keola Wong, and Bob Stauffer of ulukau.org, all knowledgeable in Hawaiian—and Jez Keighley, knowledgeable in Dutch. Staff workers at the Hawai'i State Archives, the Hawaiian Historical Society, Bernice P. Bishop Museum, the Wisconsin Historical Society, and Notre Dame University. Grateful thanks to all. And to Jane Gillespie for her sensitive work with graphics, and Dawn Sueoka for her conscientious research and fact-checking.

Contents

Timeline ~ vi

Foreword ~ xiii

Called and Chosen ~ 1

Life at Kalawao ~ 13

Unto Death ~ 63

The Making of a Saint ~ 101

Glossary ~ 117

Further Reading ~ 118

Photo Credits ~ 120

Timeline

1840	Jozef De Veuster is born on January 3, at Tremelo, in rural Belgium, the seventh of eight children in a Flemish Catholic family
1848	He goes to school at Braine-le-Comte
1850	He takes first communion
1859	He enters the House of Formation of the Congregation of the Sacred Hearts of Jesus, Mary ~~and Joseph~~ at Louvain
1860	He goes to Paris, to the mother house of the Sacred Hearts. On October 6 he takes his vows as Brother Damien
1861	Back in Louvain, he continues theological studies
1863	In February, his older brother is ordained a Sacred Hearts priest, Father Pamphile.
	In September, Damien receives minor orders
	He is chosen to join a mission to Hawai'i
	On November 8, he and fellow Sacred Hearts missionaries sail for the Pacific
1864	On March 19, their ship anchors at Honolulu
	On May 21, Damien is ordained a priest at the Cathedral of Our Lady of Peace in Honolulu, and on May 22 he celebrates his first Mass
	On June 7, he sails to the island of Hawai'i, to take up work in his first parish, Puna

Timeline

1865 — With the incurable disease of leprosy becoming epidemic in the Islands, a law is passed to segregate sufferers at a settlement at Kalawao, on a remote promontory on the island of Molokaʻi

1866 — In January, the first shipload of sufferers is landed at the settlement

On Hawaiʻi, Damien sees leprosy in Puna and in his later parish districts, Hāmākua and Kohala

1873 — Attending the blessing of a church on the island of Maui, Damien volunteers to serve as the resident priest of Kalawao

On May 10, he steps ashore at the settlement

He sleeps under a puhala (pandanus) tree until he can build himself a house, 16' x 10'

Throughout the 1870s, more and more sufferers are shipped to the settlement. The population at Kalawao and Kalaupapa is 700 or more, even with deaths at between 100 and 200 a year

1874 — King Kalākaua and Queen Kapiʻolani briefly visit the settlement

1876 — Damien enlarges St. Philomena Church

Over the years, he designs more chapels and constructs hospital buildings and orphanages

1879 — For the first time, a resident doctor is appointed, but does not stay long

Most months of most years, Damien is alone as a priest, and is without a confessor

1881 — In September, Damien is decorated with the Royal Order of Kalakaua

From 1881–1884 there is no resident doctor at the settlement

1883 — Franciscan sisters arrive in Honolulu to serve at the leprosy receiving station at Kakaʻako

A German microbiologist, Dr. Eduard Arning, is hired by the Board of Health to study leprosy scientifically

Timeline

1884	A part-Hawaiian leprosy sufferer, Ambrose Hutchison, becomes superintendent of the settlement
	In May, Dr. Arthur Mouritz is appointed resident doctor
	In July, Queen Kapiʻolani, Princess Liliʻuokalani, and Dr. Arning visit the settlement. Arning takes photographs. Kapiʻolani corresponds with Damien about help for patients
	In September, Arning examines Damien
	In October, the author Charles Warren Stoddard visits the settlement; in 1885, he publishes a book about Damien which becomes known worldwide
1885	In January, Damien is examined by Arning, and there is clear evidence of leprosy
	In May, he is again examined; the presence of leprosy is confirmed
1886	On March 30, Damien's name is entered on the official Board of Health register as a diagnosed sufferer
	In July, Ira B. Dutton comes to the settlement to assist Damien, who names him Brother Joseph
1887	More and more leprosy sufferers are shipped to the settlement. The population rises to 1,000 by the end of the decade
	Damien's condition worsens considerably; he is disfigured, but continues working nonstop
1888	In January, a severe storm blows the steeple off St. Philomena Church. Damien sets about rebuilding
	In November, Mother Marianne Cope and two Franciscan sisters, Leopoldina Burns and Mary Vincentia McCormick, come to live and work at the settlement—a great reinforcement
	Also arriving at the settlement are two more priests and a lay brother

Timeline

1889 — Damien's condition worsens, approaching terminal

March 19 is the twenty-fifth anniversary of his arrival in Hawai'i

On March 28 he becomes bed-ridden and can no longer leave his house

He dies on April 15, and is buried by the puhala tree where he slept when he first came to the settlement

In May, the world-famous author Robert Louis Stevenson visits the settlement; he becomes a strong advocate of Damien as worthy of consideration for sainthood

1895 — In France, a Sacred Hearts sister, Simplicia Hue, apparently terminally ill, prays to Damien, and experiences an overnight cure, living another 32 years. This is the basis of a first miracle attributable to Damien, leading to proceedings to beatify him

1918 — Mother Marianne dies

1931 — Joseph Dutton dies, after 45 years at the settlement

1932 — Ambrose Hutchison dies, after 53 years at the settlement, having handwritten a long memoir

By this time, Kalawao has been abandoned and the settlement has moved to Kalaupapa

1936 — Damien's coffin is exhumed and his remains are transported to Belgium, where he is reinterred at the Church of St. Anthony in Louvain

In Honolulu, Audrey Toguchi, a second-grader, sees the procession in the street outside Our Lady of Peace Cathedral

Timeline

1938	Beatification proceedings are begun
1955	Pope Pius XII approves the introduction of the Cause of the Servant of God, Father Damien
1957	Mele Meheula dies after 69 years at the settlement, the last patient with living memories of Damien
1959	Another stage in the beatification process is reached with a decree issued to the Congregation of the Causes of Saints
1965	The State Legislature of Hawai'i names Damien as one of two eminent and illustrious leaders whose statues will be placed in Statuary Hall in the national capitol in Washington, D.C.
1969	The Damien statue is unveiled in Washington. A replica stands outside the state capitol in Honolulu
	The policy of compulsory segregation at the settlement is ended. Modern medicine has rendered it no longer necessary, and the incidence of the disease in Hawai'i has declined to almost zero
1977	Pope Paul VI declares Damien of heroic virtue, venerable. Damien's annual feast day is to be May 10, the date of his landing at the settlement
1980	Kalaupapa is designated a National Historic Park
1984	Mother Teresa writes to Pope John Paul II saying Damien could be the saint to inspire work among leprosy sufferers worldwide
1991	The cure of Sister Simplicia Hue is accepted as a miracle, further clearing the path for the beatification of Damien
1992	Pope John Paul II issues the decree of beatification
1995	On June 4, the pope beatifies Damien at a ceremony in Brussels
	The bones of Damien's right hand are returned to Kalaupapa as a holy relic and are reinterred at St. Philomena Church
1998	Audrey Toguchi, diagnosed with incurable cancer in Honolulu, has gone twice to Kalaupapa to pray at Damien's tomb, and X-rays over the following months show that her cancer has disappeared completely. A professional medical account of her case becomes the basis for investigation of a possible second miracle attributable to Damien, opening the way to the process of canonization

Timeline

2008 The second miracle is formally recognized

 In June, the Congregation of the Causes of Saints recommends that Damien be canonized

 In July, Pope Benedict XVI promulgates a decree officially verifying the miracle

2009 In February, the date for the canonization ceremony is set, October 11

 In March, President Barack Obama signs into law a bill authorizing the organization Ka ʻOhana O Kalaupapa to establish the Kalaupapa Memorial, recording the names of all those sent to the settlement—about 8,000

 By this time, the population of the settlement is down to just a few dozen

 On October 6, the United States Senate passes a resolution recognizing Damien and his work

 On October 11, in Rome, Damien is canonized—Saint Damien

Damien's statue at the Hawai'i State Capitol building in Honolulu.

Foreword

This book is about the making of Saint Damien.

His life began humbly. He was born Jozef De Veuster, in 1840, at Tremelo in rural Belgium, hardworking farm country. His family was Catholic, Flemish-speaking. Jozef was the seventh of eight children. Two of his older sisters and an older brother went into the Church. At 18, Jozef joined his brother, Pamphile, in the Congregation of the Sacred Hearts of Jesus, Mary and Joseph. He took Damien as his name in religion.

At 23, not yet a priest, he volunteered for a mission to the Hawaiian Islands. He was ordained at Honolulu in 1864 and was assigned to the island of Hawaii.

An epidemic of leprosy was spreading among native Hawaiians. The disease was devastating—physically horrible, incurable. Damien saw it, and was moved.

In 1865, the Board of Health of the Hawaiian Kingdom established a settlement at Kalawao, an isolated place on a promontory on the remote island of Molokai. Sufferers were rounded up by armed police and shipped away, condemned to serve the life sentence of their disease out of sight, in exile.

At Kalawao there was no law, and no hope, only disfigurement and death.

In 1873, Damien volunteered to go to the settlement. He was 33. He spent the rest of his life serving the doomed people of Kalawao, hundreds of them, rising to a thousand.

For much of the time he was alone as a priest, and most of the time there was no resident doctor, and next to no government. Damien did what needed to be done—which amounted to everything. With his own hands, and with whatever help he could muster, he built churches and hospitals. He bandaged sores, baptized converts, administered last rites, hammered together coffins, and dug graves. He planted and harvested food crops. He took care of orphans, and managed every kind of problem for sufferers who could not manage for themselves.

Damien offered himself to the people of Kalawao, body and soul. Then leprosy took him. He was diagnosed at the turn of 1884–1885; the disease ran its course, and he died in 1889, aged 49.

He died famous. Kalawao, away in the vastness of the northern Pacific, was as obscure as any place on earth, and Damien had no wish for celebrity—"I would desire to remain unknown." But he did become known, and after he contracted the disease he was greatly celebrated. His death made headlines worldwide.

Foreword

The newspapers of the day were ready to declare him a saint on the spot. The church took longer. Necessarily: for sainthood, there must be two miracles, the first for beatification, the second for canonization, both scrupulously authenticated.

The first miracle came in 1895. A Sacred Hearts sister in France, Simplicia Hue, was deathly ill. She prayed to Damien to intercede for her, and overnight she was cured, living another 32 years. Serious investigations for beatification were not begun until the 1930s. The decree was issued in 1992, and the ceremony took place in 1995, a hundred years after the cure.

A second miraculous cure came in the 1990s—and it came in Hawai'i. A part-Hawaiian woman, Audrey Toguchi, suffering from an incurable cancer, went twice to pray at Damien's gravesite, and her tumor shrank and kept shrinking until it disappeared—without treatment. There was no medical explanation.

This time the investigations went more quickly. The miracle was formally recognized in 2008, and in 2009 Damien was canonized, declared a saint.

In the 1960s, Damien was officially recognized by the State of Hawai'i as one of its two most eminent and illustrious men. His statue was installed with those of other great national figures in Statuary Hall in Washington, D.C.; a replica was given pride of place outside the capitol building in Honolulu.

By then the village of Kalawao, where he lived and worked and died, had vanished. The leprosy epidemic had burned itself out long ago, and by the mid-twentieth century, modern medicines had ended the need for physical segregation. There were still survivors at the settlement, but their numbers were small, and they lived now at Kalaupapa, across the promontory from Kalawao.

Today, Kalaupapa is a National Historic Park. The population is down to a not much more than a handful. A movement has been organized to record the names of all who were forced into exile to die at the settlement—about eight thousand—and to erect a monument to them.

Damien's gravesite is close by the Church of St. Philomena, where he celebrated Mass and served his people.

All this is fact, public fact—Damien from the outside, so to speak. How to tell his story in a way that gets as close as possible to the man?

The best way, the truest way, is also the simplest way—through his own words.

Damien's words are the heart and soul of this book, beginning with a letter to his parents when he was eight, ending with his words on his death bed. Here, on page after page, the handwritten record of his years at Kalawao is reproduced—faded ink, on ragged brittle paper, but vital testimony to his life and his labors, all the way to his innermost thoughts.

Foreword

There are photographs documenting things that Damien touched and held in his hands—his drawings for churches and his carpenter's tools for building them, a big sea shell that he used as a holy water font, his rosary, his eyeglasses, his walking stick.

There are photographs of the man himself taken during his time at the settlement. Not many, because the cameras of his day were big and bulky, heavy and clumsy, difficult to transport to hard-to-reach places like Kalawao—also because the Board of Health did not want pictures of leprosy in Hawai'i to be exhibited in the outside world. Still, there are a handful of images of Father Damien—among the boys and girls of Kalawao, his beloved children, and, at the end, on his death bed, then robed for burial.

And there are pen portraits, the words of people who saw him face to face at Kalawao: Arthur Mouritz and Eduard Arning, the doctors who diagnosed his leprosy; fellow priests of the Sacred Hearts mission; and occasional visitors who put their impressions on paper.

Two people who were with Damien every day for years wrote about what they saw in him. Joseph Dutton, an American, came to work at the settlement in 1886. He was Damien's right hand, and very observant. Ambrose Hutchison, a part-Hawaiian, was rounded up and shipped to Kalawao as a young man, in 1879. He was close to Damien for ten years, until Damien's death. Hutchison lived on at Kalawao, for more than half a century in all, dying in 1932. He handwrote a long memoir—invaluable eyewitness testimony. And Leopoldina Burns, an Irish Franciscan sister who came to Kalawao in Damien's last days, filled many notebooks with her vivid memories.

There are letters back and forth between Damien and Hawaiian royalty. There are the words of two popes: John Paul II, who beatified him, and Benedict XVI, who canonized him.

There are the words of world figures who have found inspiration in Damien: Gandhi, Mother Teresa, President Franklin Delano Roosevelt, President Barack Obama. And Audrey Toguchi, who prayed to Damien and was healed.

And there are the words of those who were closest of all to Damien: his people, the Hawaiian leprosy sufferers of Kalawao, putting their needs and hopes and fears on paper in their homely handwriting, placing their faith in Father Damien, "Makua Damiano," in the certainty that he would do everything he could to help them—that he would give his life for them.

Note: In Damien's time, everyone used the word "leper"—including Damien himself. Accordingly, in quotations taken directly fromt those times, the word is retained. In our day, use of the word is discouraged, because it stigmatizes sufferers.

Damien at 23—a photograph taken for his family just before he left on the Sacred Hearts mission to Hawai'i.

CALLED AND CHOSEN
1840–1873

J. Damien cath p.
born Jan 3rd 1840

Damien was called to be a missionary. From an early age, he wanted to do God's work in some distant place.

The Sacred Hearts had a mission to the Pacific. In 1863, Damien, 23 years old and still not an ordained priest, volunteered to go to Hawai'i.

In May 1864, he was ordained at Our Lady of Peace Cathedral in Honolulu. He celebrated his first Mass there, and in June he sailed to the island of Hawai'i to take up his priestly work in the field.

Hawai'i could not have been more different from his home country. Belgium was a cold, flat land. Hawai'i was tropical, spectacularly beautiful, with high mountains, deep valleys, and waterfalls; and Damien's first parish district, Puna, had an active volcano, Kīlauea, whose firepit, Halema'uma'u, put him in mind of hell.

His second parish, Kohala–Hāmākua, was huge—more than a thousand square miles—and physically demanding. He had to climb mountains and cross ravines. Once, out on the water along the coast, his canoe overturned and he had to swim for his life. He spent weeks at a time on horseback, packing a portable altar; as he put it, his home was in the saddle.

He built small chapels, taught the catechism, and was an energetic converter and baptizer—the busiest of missionary priests, driving his strong healthy body to the limit, delighting in the labor.

He came to know Hawaiians, and to like them greatly. "Service among Christians you love and who love you tied us by powerful bonds."

He lived and worked on the island of Hawai'i for nine years. Leprosy was there before him. He saw it in its awfulness: "There are many men covered with it." The police were rounding up sufferers for shipping to Kalawao. Damien was moved to write: "I can only attribute to God an undeniable feeling that soon I shall join them."

He is Called

Damien—

My dear parents:

I cannot but write to you on this beautiful Christmas Day which has brought me to the certainty that God wants me to abandon the world and embrace religious life. Do not think I do this to indulge myself. It is Divine Providence who has prepared me. If God calls me, I must obey.

I hope that my turn will come to choose the road I must walk.

I ask God, through the intercession of St. Francis Xavier, to grant me the grace to be sent one day to the missions.

Damien's birthplace, the De Veuster family home in Tremelo, Belgium (above).

At age 8, he writes to his parents—the earliest surviving letter (left).

Silence, Contemplation, God's Presence

Father Pamphile De Veuster—
Father Wenceslas had preached a sermon one day in which he emphasized three points. My brother, as if writing the words on paper was not enough, wished to have them always before his eyes, so he took his knife and cut them into the wood of his desk.

"Silence, Contemplation, God's Presence"—words for Damien the novice to remember.

Honolulu Harbor, much as Damien would have seen it on his arrival (top photo). On the island of Hawai'i, Damien's first parish, Puna, had a spectacular volcano, Kīlauea. The firepit, Halema'uma'u, put him in mind of hell (bottom photo).

DAMIEN—
Here I am a priest.

Instead of a tranquil and withdrawn life, it is a question of getting used to traveling by land and by sea; instead of strictly observing silence, it is necessary to learn to speak several languages with all kinds of people; instead of being directed you have to direct others; and the hardest of all is to preserve, in the middle of a thousand miseries and vexations, the spirit of meditation and prayer.

I have four Catholic schools which I try to oversee, and where I teach catechism.

After mass I often give a little talk. Then it is breakfast, always with poi; after that (at least for the last seven months) I take off my cassock and grab the saw. Only with a lot of sweat have I been able to build some chapels that are decent both inside and outside.

I have three wooden churches and several chapels which are thatched. I try to be in each church at least once a month on Sunday.

The last church I built is a fine-looking building with a nice little tower.

As a priest I am usually on the road, and at my rectory very little. I am, perhaps, traveling three or four out of every six weeks to visit my dear children in Christ.

It takes me six weeks to visit everyone.

Kohala

Damien—
We cannot travel here either by train or trap and not always by foot. How do you think we manage these long journeys? With good mules and excellent horses. I have just bought a superb horse for 100 francs and a mule for 75.

I have become a skilled rider. I now have two horses and two mules. I don't spend anything on these beasts. When I arrive late in the evening after having ridden 10 leagues, I tie up the horse and it looks for its own food: there is no shortage of grass.

The coast of Kohala, Damien's second parish.

When One Serves God, One Is Happy Anywhere

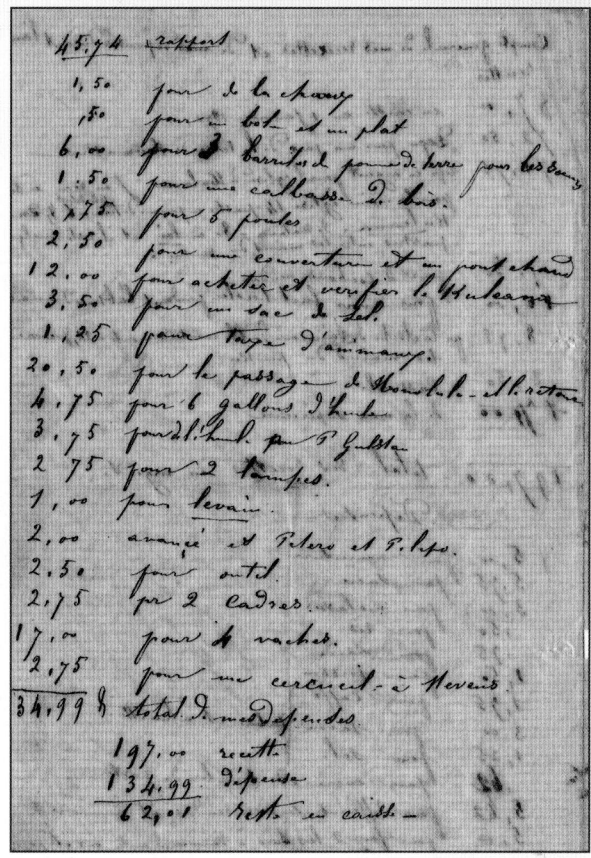

Damien—
We eat what Providence sends us. The calabash of poi is always full; there is also meat, water in quantity, coffee and bread sometimes, wine or beer never Sometimes the plates are not well washed, either, but what matter. Hunger and habit make us eat just the same. For dessert, we smoke a pipe.

I am always in the best of health. It seems to me that, physically, I am now perfectly adjusted to the active life of the missionary.

When one serves God, one is happy anywhere.

Damien kept strict accounts of his expenses, down to what he paid for five chickens.

I Like Our Poor Kanaka Very Much

People of Kohala.

You Could Not Wish for Better People

Damien—
I like our poor kanaka very much.

You could not wish for better people, gentle, pleasant-mannered, exceedingly tender-hearted, they neither seek to amass riches, or live in luxury, or dress much, but are most hospitable, and ready to deprive themselves of necessities in order to supply your every want if you have to ask a night's shelter from them.

I do all I can for them. In their turn they like me as children like their parents. It is by this mutual affection that I hope to convert them to God. For if they love the priest, they will easily love Our Lord.

Service among Christians you love and who love you tied us by powerful bonds.

I will give my life with pleasure for them, just as our Savior did.

Leprosy Is Beginning to Be Very Prevalent

Dr. Arthur Mouritz—
About the year 1864 the large increase in the number of lepers commenced to agitate the mind of the community.

Damien—
Leprosy is beginning to be very prevalent here. There are many men covered with it.

Dr. Arthur Mouritz—
Steps were taken to adopt measures to check the spread of the disease, and the law of segregation was enacted in January, 1865.

He Kanawai E Kaohi Ai I Ka Laha Ana O Ka Mai Lepera
An Act to Prevent the Spread of Leprosy—
Section 3. The Board of Health or its agents are authorized and empowered to cause to be isolated and confined, in some place or places for that purpose provided, all leprous patients who shall be deemed capable of spreading the disease of Leprosy.

Evidence of the disease.

Damien—
All the leprosy victims they have been able to collect have been sent to the Settlement on Molokai as to a government prison.

Ambrose Hutchison—
Father Damien had seen much sorrow among native families. The arrest of suspects and alleged leprous persons, either a father or mother or a daughter or some other dear relative by Police Officers and led away like criminals and cast into lockups awaiting for a vessel to take them to the living grave of Kalawao, on the island of Molokai where they never hoped to see the dear ones left behind in this life. These scenes made Father Damien's heart bleed for these unfortunate people.

Damien—
I can only attribute to God an undeniable feeling that soon I shall join them.

Damien at age 33, in 1873, the year he volunteered to serve at the Kalawao settlement.

LIFE AT KALAWAO
1873–1884

J. Damien
Cath. priest

Damien volunteered to go to Kalawao in May 1873. The settlement was on a bare promontory, pounded by surf and walled in on the landward side by a pali, a cliff of more than a thousand feet—a natural prison.

Conditions were dreadful: hundreds of sufferers covered in sores, dead bodies left lying, pigs and dogs scavenging amongst the corpses. There was drunkenness and rioting. The Hawaiians had a saying: "In this place there is no law."

With nowhere to live, Damien slept under a puhala, a pandanus tree, until he could build himself a small house.

From the start, and never stopping, year after year, he worked fifteen-hour days and longer, beginning at 5 a.m., visiting the sick, cleaning and bandaging sores, offering last rites, making coffins, digging graves, and negotiating with the Board of Health to improve the settlement, taking charge of building hospitals, dormitories, and orphanages, laying water pipes, blasting rocks at the landing place. "A vigorous, forcefull, impellant man," Ambrose Hutchison called him.

He was a friend to all, Catholic or non-Catholic. And he was a particular friend to orphan children—his finest work, so Dr. Arthur Mouritz wrote.

He worked himself to exhaustion, "a lamp with no more oil." And he was isolated as a priest; he had no steady colleague, no regular confessor. But he found resources in himself to keep on and keep on: "This is my work in this world."

Damien impressed the rulers of the Hawaiian Kingdom, and was awarded a royal decoration. The decoration itself meant nothing to him. The people of Kalawao were everything. He offered himself to them. "I make myself a leper with the lepers, to gain all to Jesus Christ. That is why, in preaching, I say we lepers."

> *By especial Providence of our Divine Lord who During his public life showed a particular sympathy for the lepers, my way, as a catholic priest was traced towards Kalawao, in May. AD 1873.; I was then thirty three years of age, enjoying a robust good health.*

Damien—

By special Providence of our Divine Lord who during his public life showed a particular sympathy for lepers, my way as a catholic priest was traced toward Kalawao in May AD 1873. I was then thirty three years of age, enjoying a robust good health.

Robert Louis Stevenson—

The place as regards scenery is grand, gloomy and bleak. Mighty mountain walls descending sheer along the whole face of the island into a sea unusually deep; the front of the mountain ivied and furred with clinging forest, one iridescent cliff; about halfway from east to west, the low, bare, stony promontory edged in between the cliff and the ocean.

Damien's own handwritten account of the origins of his ministry at Kalawao.

Sunburnt and Dust-Colored, Blackened at the Edges

Dr. Arthur Mouritz—
The plain is in the form of a tongue of land, three sides being washed by the ocean, the fourth or continuation of the base of the tongue ending in perpendicular cliffs, washed by the sea, affording no egress, or ingress, except by boat or canoe.

Charles Warren Stoddard—
Sunburnt and dust-colored, blackened at the edges. Near the center of the lowland was a small, low crater, a hillock with a funnel-shaped hollow. The whole plain was like a crust over the water, with a broken bubble in the midst of it.

A view of Kalaupapa promontory.

Nuhou, The Hawaiian News—
Thirty lepers were landed from the Kilauea at Kalawao last Saturday, and eight doubtful leprous cases were brought to town. This leprosy is certainly the worst difficulty and most important work with which the government has to grapple.

Ambrose Hutchison—
Taken to the leper detention station adjoining the Police headquarters on King Street, and from there after being held for a time, again taken with 11 other fellow unfortunates marched through the streets of Honolulu, guarded on each side by a squad of policemen down the Esplanade at the end of Fort Street on the waterfront and put aboard of a steamer named Mokolii lying alongside appeared, which put to sea, and the following morning came to anchor in the roadstead and put into a boat as human cargo and rowed ashore, and finally dumped at the landing place, a crevice in the rock-flat and left to the tender mercies of the officials in charge of the leper settlement, such is the fate men, women and children over whom the pronouncement of a Government physician the magic word leper, sealed their doomed, these afflicted adjudged exiled for life from home and all they hold dear, to enter into a Penal Institution over its portal is inscribed the words: "He or she who enters here leave hope behind."

"Leave hope behind." Ambrose Hutchison, a part-Hawaiian, chronicles his forcible exile to Kalawao as a young man.

A Steamer Landed Me Here

DAMIEN—
His Highness expressed the wish that one of us would visit Molokai. I saw coming the realization of the project of Providence.

A steamer landed me here, together with a batch of fifty lepers whom the authorities had collected.

BISHOP LOUIS MAIGRET—
So far, my children, you have been left alone and uncared for. But you shall be no longer. Behold, I have brought you one who will be a father to you, to live and die with you. Here is Father Damien.

Nuhou, The Hawaiian News
A Christian Hero—
We have often said, that the poor outcast lepers of Molokai, without pastor or physician, afforded an opportunity for the exercise of a noble Christian heroism, and we are happy to say that the hero has been found. When the Kilauea touched at Kalawao last Saturday, Bishop Maigret and Father Damien, a Belgian priest, went ashore. The venerable Bishop addressed the lepers with many comforting words, and introduced to them the good father, who had volunteered to live with them and for them. Father Damien formed this resolution at the time and was left ashore among the lepers without a home or a change of clothing except such as the lepers offer. We care not what this man's theology may be, he is surely a Christian hero.

Damien—
May the Lord protect me from being carried away by vanity. If I am much talked about in the newspapers and in the churches, I wish that all the glory be given to the author and accomplisher of all good. I would desire to remain unknown in Kalawao.

My greatest happiness is to serve the Lord in these poor sick children, made outcasts by the rest of men.

I want to sacrifice myself for my poor lepers.

A Honolulu newspaper records Damien's arrival at the settlement—"A Christian Hero."

Damien—
No house to shelter me.

I am living under a Puuhala (that is to say, a pandanus) while waiting for the lumber to build a house.

Ambrose Hutchison—
This Puhala tree and spot was dear to the heart of Father Damien as the kind sheltering friend of those first eventfull weeks of his mission.

Damien—
The whites of Honolulu, having assisted me with their donations, I was able to build myself a hut, sixteen feet long and ten wide.

I Came to Molokai Without Bringing Anything with Me

DAMIEN—
I came to Molokai without bringing anything with me.

Send me a case of wine, some spiritual books and others for studying, some shirts, trousers, shoes, the bell, rosaries, catechisms, altar bread, small and large, a bag of flour, and a lockbox.

I would appreciate a sack of rice, a supply of coffee, and a mule as soon as they can be sent; also a horse with saddle and bridle.

P.S. Don't forget to inquire about the chest with 4 drawers where my tools and clothes are. This is the fourth week since I have been without a change of clothes.

A Royal Visit

Damien—
Last Tuesday I was just about to climb the pali when the king and his entourage arrived.

Pacific Commercial Advertiser—
The King and Queen landed at 12:30 and were received by the assembled patients with hearty cheers. The King made a short but feeling address. After a few words of kindly recognition to personal acquaintances, and a general "Aloha oukou," their Majesties returned to the steamer, painfully affected with the sights of human affliction that they had witnessed.

King David Kalākaua visited Kalawao with his wife, Queen Kapi'olani, shortly after ascending the throne in 1874.

Damien—
I live alone.

As for my meals, I eat only two a day, rarely have a midday meal.

In the morning, after Mass, a woman who is clean of the disease comes to get my food ready. My meal consists of rice, meat, coffee, and sometimes ship-biscuits. In the evening, for supper, I eat leftovers with a cup of tea that I heat with my lamp.

Joseph Manu—
Father Damien warmed up his food a few times to make another meal rather than throw anything away.

Damien—
In my leisure time I cultivate a little piece of ground, to provide food for my chickens, who in their turn provide me with food in the shape of eggs.

I live abundantly; I don't suffer from hunger.

Damien—
I am very happy and very well; in fact, I feel stronger than I ever did before.

G. W. Woods—
In the prime of life, and the perfection of youthful health and vigor.

His face was smooth and rather thin, but not emaciated, and his features irradiated by an almost constant humorous smile, transiently ceasing to leave an earnest impression intensified by a fixed gaze of calm dark eyes. The chin slightly projected, with a deep sulcus below thick, widely parted lips, and the head, poised upon rather a long neck, was covered with thick black curly hair carelessly brushed or unbrushed. He wore a soutan which had seen much wear and tear and not been too well cared for.

Ambrose Hutchison—
A well knit stocky man of medium height, dark hair, prominent straight nose, plump round smooth face and wearing gold rim spectacles, garbed in black cassock with a rope girdle of the same color around his waist, on his head a black furr stiff brim hat held by four bands on the crown, his right held the curved end of a stout cane and the other hand held his folded stola, walk across the yard and threw the gate on to the road and up to where I stood and in Hawaiian greeted, "Aloha maikai oe." I reciprocated: "Aloha maikai oe, e ka makua." He ask my name, where I come from and with whom I lived. Answering his queries, we stood talking familiarly like old friends for a while, before going invited to call on him at his residence which I did later; he walk away, I looking after him, consciously impressed, muttered to myself—here is another found friend.

Dr. Arthur Mouritz—
His good physical development enabled him to work for hours with little fatigue.

Ambrose Hutchison—
A vigorous, forceful, impellant man.

Damien—
Manual work is very good for my health, and I feel well and happy among my unfortunate sick people.

There is enough to do to keep a priest busy from morning to night.

Ambrose Hutchison—
The number of lepers living in the Leper Asylum of Kalawao on the first day of January 1873, according to official record were 303 males and 156 females, and brought to the Settlement during the year an addition of 488 lepers (293 males and 195 females) totaling 947 lepers (596 males and 351 females) and death took 115 (75 males and 40 females).

Most of Them Live in Little Huts

DAMIEN—
The Kalaupapa landing place was at that time a somewhat deserted village of three or four wooden cottages and a few old grass houses. The lepers were allowed to go there only on the days when a vessel arrived; they were living at Kalawao. All the other lepers, with a very few kokua (helpers), had taken their abode further up towards the valley. They had cut down the old pandanus or puu hala groves to build their houses; though a great many had nothing but branches of castor oil trees to construct their small shelters. These frail frames were covered in with ki leaves, sugar cane leaves, the best ones with grass. Under such primitive roofs were living pell mell, without distinction of ages or sexes, old or new cases, all more or less strangers one to another, those unfortunate outcasts of society. They passed their time with playing cards, hula, drinking fermented ki root beer, Homemade alcohol, and with the sequels of all this.

My poor people continually ask me to help them put up a little wooden house.

Most of them live in little huts which those who still have intact hands and feet build.

The Government supply the framework, the mission provides planks and then they are covered with grass or sugar cane leaves. I usually give them a hand for a few days and lo and behold they have accommodation.

Hawaiian dwellings in the settlement district.

I Built a New Church

KAILI—
I have this day sold my tool box and all the tools contained therein to the Rev. Father Damien for the sum of $10.

DAMIEN—
I am busy making a good cabinet for the sacristy where the vestments will be safe. So have no fear of sending an assortment of nice mass vestments and some church linen with a chalice and ciborium. Don't forget a bit of white silk for the tabernacle.

Pray for us.

I would like to make 5 or 6 pews but I have no more lumber. 200 ft. of lumber, appropriate for this purpose, please.

I have just built another chapel, at the other end of the settlement.

In two weeks there won't be many nails left to be pounded into place. Then comes the painting. Please, send me a bell and a pretty painting for the altar, as well as a supply of all colors of paint, either in powder form or in cans. Chrome, red, green, blue, yellow, brown.

I built a new church at our harbor—and took done the other one—which is now in a neighborhood outside the leprosie. Thus I now have again 3 churches to attend to all this winter season.

During the winter I worked hard to enlarge my church and build a pretty tower.

The tools of Damien the carpenter (top photos). A tireless builder, he reports on his activities in English—which was not his best language (bottom photo).

Life at Kalawao

Father Damien Again Donned His Work Clothes

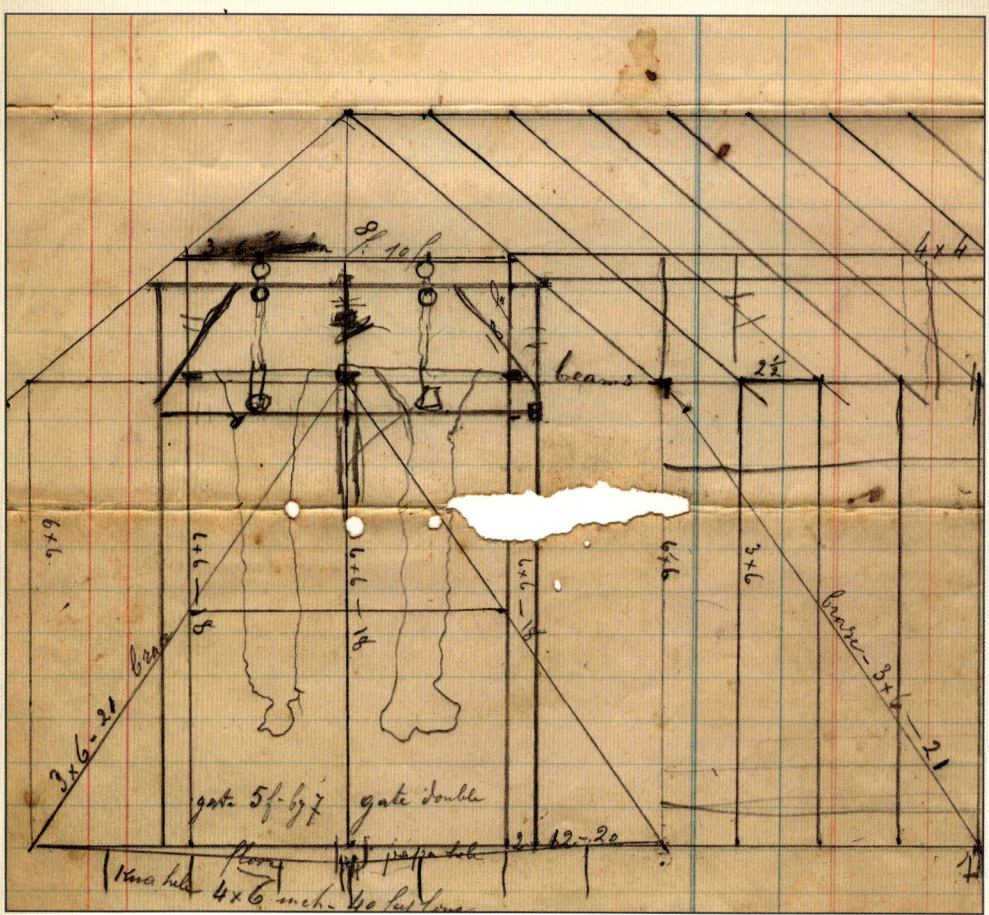

Ambrose Hutchison—
Father Damien again donned his work clothes and with his helper started work on the addition to the chapel in accordance with his plan and some weeks of steady work Father Damien had the satisfaction of seeing the carpenter work on the exterior of the new building with its tall steeple pointed skyward completed.

They continued to work steadily for some weeks longer to finish what carpentering work remained undone. With the carpenter work finished in good workmanship in every detail the handy work of a master mechanic. Painters applied paint on the finished wood work in and out in varied hue with finishing touches of colors here and there the beautiful little church was ready for dedication to the services of God which the village of Kalawao was fortunate to have in its midst.

Plans for a church.

Damien—
No, I am not ashamed to be a bricklayer or a carpenter when it is for the glory of God!

Charles Warren Stoddard—
We saw the little chapel and most of the private dwellings where families live; the girls' home with a new dining room that Father Damien has been putting up with his own hands, and the few remaining grass huts which are occupied by the older natives.

St. Philomena Church, with a steeple added by Damien (top photo). The costs of building (bottom photo).

Life at Kalawao

G. W. Woods—
Father Damien was architect, constructor, carpenter and painter, instructing and working, and yet finding time to attend the sick and dying, dress the hundreds of mutilated beings who came to him for salve and bandages, besides conscientiously administering every holy office of the church. He also inculcated temperance, sexual morals, family life, the avoidance of gambling, cleanliness of person and attire, and instructed the people in gardening, cooking, and many little household arts, adding greatly to their comfort.

Kalawao in the 1870s.

J. Kalani, Kaneone Kekaa, Joken Kaluna, Aberahama—
We the undersigned cordially agree to live in peace under Father Damien.

We will never again go out at night, and be attentive as to how we conduct ourselves—and that with God's power to help us.

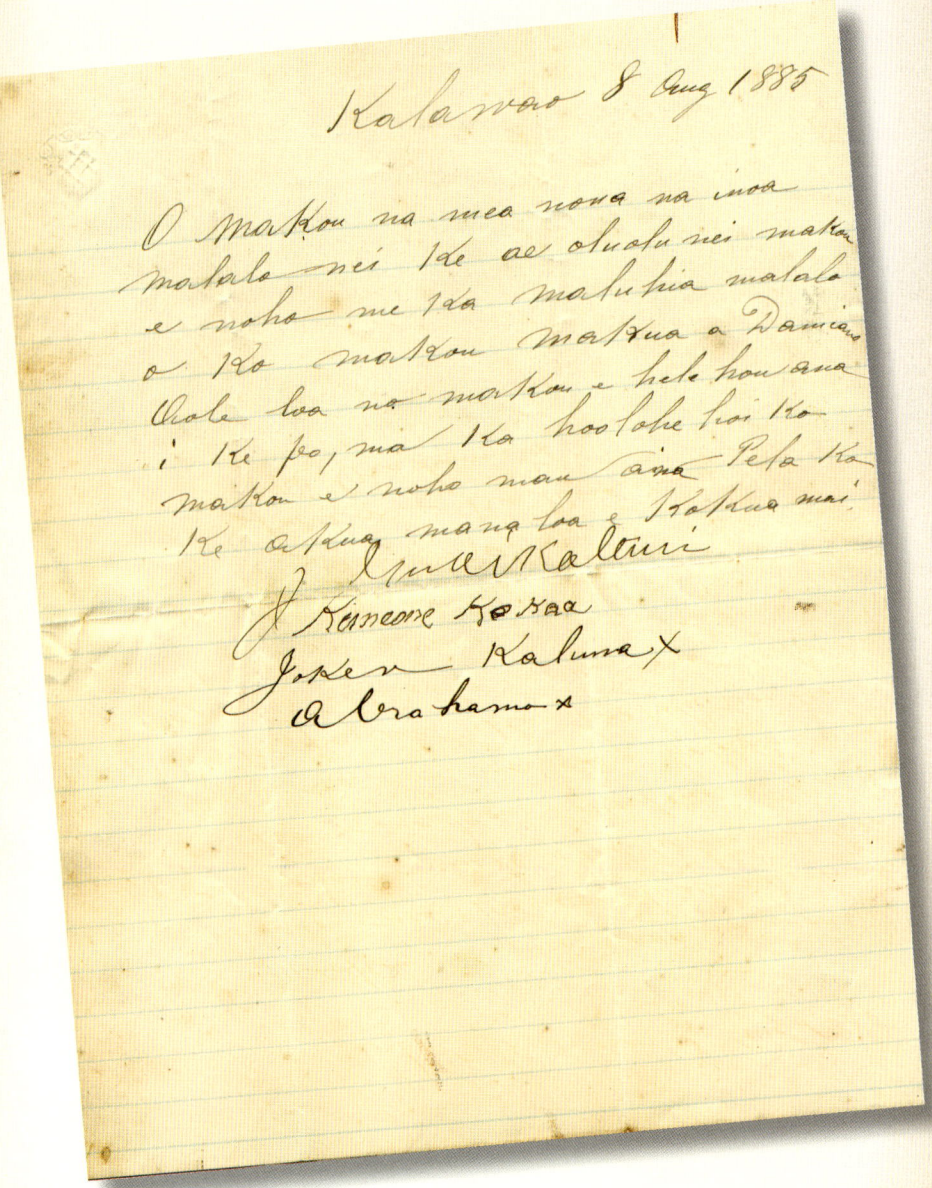

Damien persuading four men at the settlement to "live in peace." Two of them make their mark with an X.

I Make Myself a Leper

Damien—
I like working at the chapels, but I like working at the conversion of my poor lepers even more.

I make myself a leper with the lepers, to gain all to Jesus Christ. That is why, in preaching, I say we lepers, not my brethren, as in Europe.

Damien—
Prière
Juin 26, 1873

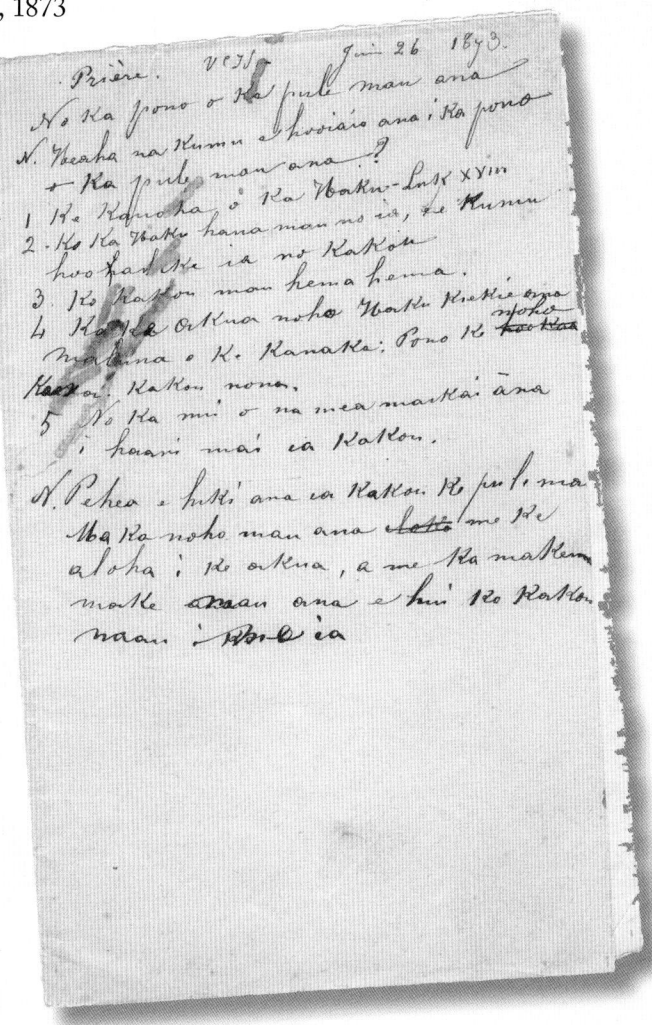

Damien's notes for a prayer—in Hawaiian, the language in which he preached and spoke to his people.

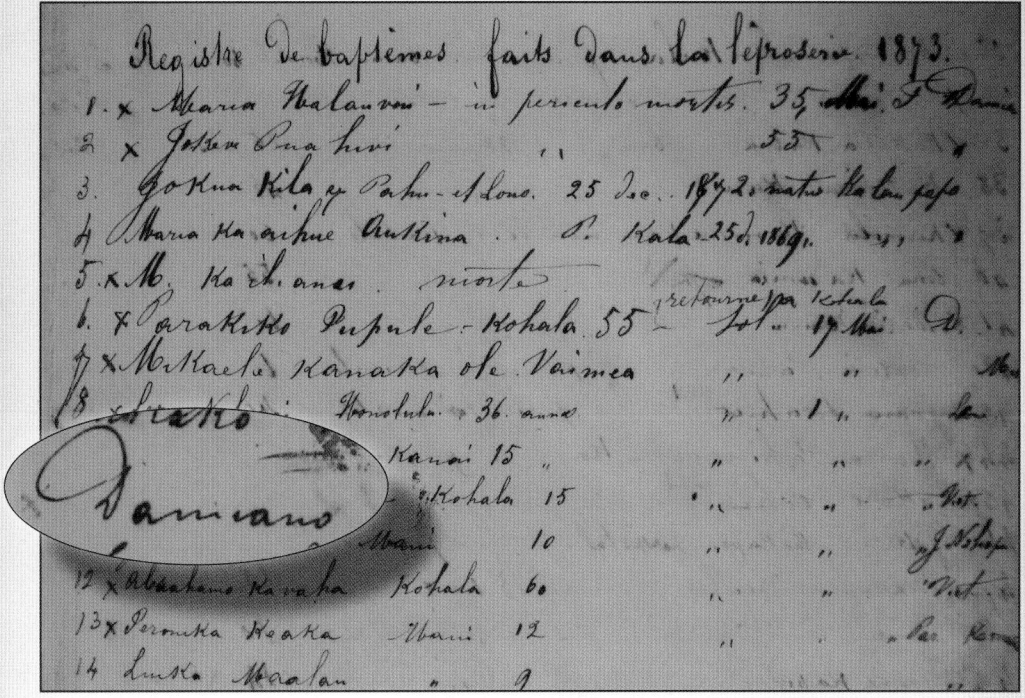

Damien—
During the Pascal season, I have had lots of consolation at the leprosarium—many confessions and communions, 32 baptisms and 11 death-bed confessions, and almost all administered during the 8 days of Easter week. On Easter itself, solemn blessing of the cemetery and the beautiful cross, with drums and music leading the procession.

Ambrose Hutchison—
He never neglected his priestly duties, visiting on the sick and dying, and immediate call for him while hard at work, drop his tool, pull off his work clothes and put on his cassock and his stola in hand and hastened to the dying to administer the last rite of the church.

The Kalawao baptismal registry. From Damien's first year at the settlement, 1873, the baptismal name Damiano appears.

Damien—
In tears I sow the good seed among my poor lepers. I am amidst heartbreaking physical and moral misery.

Dr. Eduard Arning—
We gather together very nearly a thousand suffering people in a lonely spot and let them have only a flying visit of a doctor once a month!

Chalice, vestment, holy water font. Damien often served Mass several times a day.

Damien—

They poor people were without any medicines, with the exception of a few phisies, and their own native remedies. It was a common sight to see people going around with fearful ulcers which for the want of a few rags, or a piece of lint, and a little salve, were left exposed to dirt, flies and vermin.

A good many of the sick and prostrated were left lying there to take care of themselves and plenty of them died for want of assistance.

Dr. George L. Fitch—

Dante's Inferno contains no horrors worse than Kalawao.

Damien—

Still, I try to appear always gay, so as to raise the courage of my patients. I present death to them as the end of their ills, if they will make a sincere conversion. Many of them see their last hour come with resignation, some with joy.

Most all wishes to die Catholics, and I do all I can to prepare them well—It is in this work I find my greatest consolation.

Damien—
I have so much work to do that I'm hardly ever home.

M. Loo—
Damien, Father of the Lepers.
Dear Father:

Good Father, please see the Superintendent of the Leper Settlement and ask him to furnish a new boat for bringing the freight from the steamer to the landing.

The old boat was wrecked and there is nothing the natives could do now.

Give us an immediate reply so that we know what steps to take in the matter.

The captain of the steamer will not send its boat to the landing for fear of the breakers.

Only the old timers know where to come in. There were times that we could not get our food stuff from the steamer and now our boat was wrecked. I am afraid that we take this matter very seriously.

Best regards and good luck.

For Fear of the Breakers

The landing at Kalaupapa.

Maria Manuel—

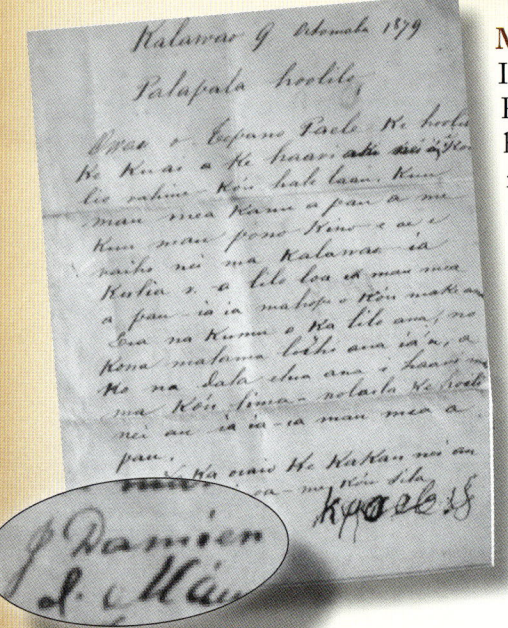

I, Maria Manuel, do hereby appoint Father Damien to take charge of my house after my death. He shall settle my affairs and convey the house to my husband.

All persons who have supported me during my life shall be paid (from fund derived from my property) by Father Damien; and if there is any balance to be paid to my husband and the Catholic Church.

J. Pilipili—
Dear Father and Friend:
Please give the sum of One Dollar and a Half to Kao for the month.

Kalaiku—
Dear Father Damien:
This is to inform you that Kelai owes $12 to me. Please tell him to pay me the above amount.

If he pays you, give the money to Aahu who is coming back to Honolulu.

S.M. Kauluaau, A. W. B. Nahakualii—
Dear Father:
We strongly protest the practice of putting our meat on the hearse and bringing it to the settlement.

We do not like this practice and we leave this matter in your hands for settlement.

Damien took on innumerable duties among Hawaiians at the settlement. Here he witnesses a will.

NAKAMIA—
Dear Beloved Father in Christ:

If it is not asking you too much, I would like you to see Poahinui and ask him as to the price of his colt.

Someone is willing to buy, provided, the price is reasonable.

Don't fail to anser.

WAHINEAUKAI—
Dear Rev. Father Damien:

I direct you to take charge of all the property of my father Hulihee and don't let anyone to take anything that belongs to my said father.

When I get out of jail, I intend to come there and settle this matter.

In the meantime, please send my letter to the following address:

Mr. Wahineaukai
Honolulu Jail,
Honolulu, Oahu.

P.S. I am the only surviving children of Hulihee.

Business dealings with Honolulu.

DAMIEN—
To Kalaola,
Honokahau.

Dear Sir:
Having been appointed as Acting Superintendent of the Leper Settlement by the Board of Health for the past few days, I hereby instruct Kawiki, Capeno Keenipulu to go and get your poi.

A. Kuokoa told me that there are 500 bags of poi.

I am ordering the poi from you. Send fresh poi and don't send any sour poi. The order is for 500 bags of poi.

You tell your son to prepare the poi on Monday and send it by steamer on Tuesday.

Fill each bag properly so that it will get here in good condition.

If your poi is good and reasonable no doubt you will always get our order.

As to the price of the poi this is between you and Bill Ragsdale.

We can order up to 1600 bags of poi for the people here.

KEAKA—
Father Damien:
Please give some undershirts to Thomas and Nakaiwalu, both of whom are helpers to the people of this house.

There are no other helpers besides them.

(Opposite page) Damien's "Personal Rule"—the daily routine of a dedicated priest.

Damien—

5 a.m. Get up—go to the church as soon as possible. Morning prayer–adoration and meditation until 6:30, Thanksgiving till a quarter to eight. Then take care of one and another thing for the good of the faithful. 8 o'clock breakfast—followed by a little talk and other business. 9 o'clock—small hours, under the waranda. 9:30 spiritual reading followed by study or letter-writing till noon: 12 o'clock lunch. After lunch visit the sick and the Christians in general—so as to see every week all that goes on in each house in my district—if I can get back by 5 o'clock—say vespers and do housework. 6 o'clock. Dinner. At first dusk rosary breviary—and evening prayer. Between 8 and 10 o'clock bed.

Kindness to all, charity to the needy, a sympathizing hand to the sufferers and the dying, in conjunction with a solid religious instruction to my listeners, have been my constant means to introduce moral habits among the lepers.

To Imitate Jesus Christ's Poverty

Ambrose Hutchison—
A man of deep faith. Preached faith and hope with all ardor of his soul.

Damien—
As a religious I must be poor in spirit, in desire, in deed. To imitate Jesus Christ's poverty more closely, I will ask only for what is strictly necessary and useful, never for what is pleasant and superfluous. I will never complain if at times I am denied what I ask for. I will think twice before buying things that are more or less necessary for me. I will keep a strict account and I will never use any trickery to get what I desire from my Superiors. I will simply ask and never order. As for the little bit obtained through the work or help of the Christians I will take only what is necessary and give the rest to the poor.

Inmost thoughts—Damien's "Imitation of Christ."

Managing Money

L'argent en reserve 5 juin 1880

55	Otu
17	Kini Kake
9.25	manini
4.	Kiwi
50	Oho
13	maka ala
4.50	Hoomanawanui
3.	Kalua
10	Makaleka
2.	Kaili
4.50	Keawinan
17.	Julia
4.50	Zakeu
4.50	Pilomena
2.	Naholowa
6.75	Pahia
6	eglise
12	Marie manuel
2.	lile
3	Kalua punana
10	monika
10	ohana
10	magasin
260.00	du. et j'ai 268.60 — en caisse rest 8

Managing money for the people of the settlement.

Ambrose Hutchison—
Daily labor without expectation of earthly reward.

Pohaku Melemaikea—
He was very humble, very modest and simple.

Kaili'ohe Kame'ekua—
Father Damien was a quiet man who never yelled at us, or seemed to get angry at us. We loved him. We all wanted him to stay with us but he always got on his donkey and rode away. He explained that Jesus never had a home or a bed, and, like Jesus, he would travel from place to place telling people about the love our heavenly father had for us.

Damien—
This is my work in this world.

Opposite: A child sentenced to life with leprosy.

Dr. Arthur Mouritz—
There were many orphans at the Leper Settlement in the care of Kokua families, but most were cared for by the Catholic mission, under the supervision of Father Damien, at Kalawao, and I claim that this was one of the finest works that this priest undertook and carried out.

Mele Meheula—
He showed his love by taking care of orphans.

I know this because I was one of them.

D. K. H. Koohokalolo—
Dear Father:
I respectfully request your kindness to accept my son James Koohokalolo, former altar boy for Father Leonor at Kakaako.

There are no signs of leprosy on him as you see him yourself.

I trust that you will take good care of him.

Victoria—
Dear Rev. Father Damien:
I arrived here for the purpose of ascertaining whether my sons Paul Kahaulomoku and Ahinui are alive or dead.

The rumor was that they are dead.

A reply to the above will be greatly appreciated.

JOHN—
Mr. Damien:
If your kindness permits, good father of the fatherless children of Kalawao, I am inquiring about the condition of a certain boy by the name of Kapoliola, who was taken from here to Kalawao, how he is getting along and whether he has some clothes or not.

If you happen to see him, please give him the aloha (love) of his grandparents and the family.

P.S. Please reply to this letter this week

S. HOOPII—
Dear Rev. Father J. Damien:
It was a rather hard parting when I left you and the family. I shall not forget the love and the good deeds you have done for the family. You are a real and true Father, a patient Father and a loving Father.

Damien at the dormitories—one of his unending responsibilities.

The List of My Orphan Children

[Handwritten letter in French, dated Kalawao, 30 Août 1883, addressed to Monseigneur Hermann, listing names of orphan boys and girls, both Catholic and non-Catholic, baptized and non-baptized.]

DAMIEN—

As we have here a good number of minor children without parents who are somewhat as vagabonds, I take the liberty of requesting the board of health, who has the full control over them, to do me the honor of intrusting to my official care and to give me a general guardianship over them.

I take the liberty of submitting to Your Excellency the list of my orphan children whom I have adopted while asking you to be so kind as to help me, in accord with the extent of your resources, to procure them what they need.

Damien makes a list for his bishop of the boys and girls in his care, Catholic and non-Catholic, baptized and non-baptized.

His Keen Personal Interest in the Welfare of His Charges

Ambrose Hutchison—
They were a happy and contented lot. His keen personal interest in the welfare of his charges had much to do with it.

Dr. Arthur Mouritz—
Fr. Damien at times joined in frolics with the "kids," skip the rope, tag me not, hide and go seek, "buff" the blind man, etc., were all entered into with childish glee.

The good father with some of the children of the settlement.

Joseph Dutton—
The small boys, and some of the larger ones too, any who are yet spry, have a great way with their games. For about a week they will play at nothing but ball—then whatever any of them introduces next, say stilts, will be all the go for the next week; then a week of kites, then of arrows, then of marbles, and so on, like boys the world over.

Ambrose Hutchison—
When not visiting the sick would take his able bodied boys to work for an hour or two and by example show them how to do it with more of a will of play than of real work.

The boys had their land walled in and set apart by the then Government for the use of lepers desiring dry farming, cleared of weeds grubed and planted with sweet potatoes, onions, cabbages and bananas. Father Damien kept his boys busy at this work, a healthy exercise for the boys that kept them from mischief and indolence.

Charles Warren Stoddard—
We went over to his work, he wishing to direct the boys, who were lying about doing nothing, and after a little the angelus rang. He knelt bareheaded among the lepers and among them said the angelus domini, all of them kneeling bareheaded among the bananas in the sun. Is this not pleasing in the sight of God?

The Kalawao Band

The boys composed a Hawaiian Song in honor of Father Damien which they sang on certain occasion. The boys had no string Instruments guitars or ukuleles as it cannot be had in the long past years, but the boys had Fifes pipe flutes Tenor and Bass drums, Triangle and Boys *[...]* music on, and named *The Kalawao Band* a Hawaiian National *[...]* boys plan to give their honored and respected Reverend Father a rousing surprised Serenade of music and songs before the Church bell ring calling the faithfulls to the early morning Mass. To this hour the boys turn out with their Instruments and station themselves in front of Father Damien house. The playing of a stirring lively tune on their tin flutes, tinkling steel *[...]* rattling bones and clashing booms of the drums, break out on the silent morning air, that aroused not only Father Damien but the whole neighborhood *[...]* rune from their prayer *[...]* ickly dress and rushed to

Damien loved music and sang well. The boys of his Kalawao Band composed a song for him. Ambrose Hutchison captures the scene.

The Boys Composed a Hawaiian Song in Honor of Father Damien

Ambrose Hutchison—
The boys composed a Hawaiian song in honor of Father Damien which they sing on certain occasion. The boys had no string instruments like guitars, ukuleles or fiddles but the boys had tin pipe flutes, tenor and bass drums, steel triangle and bones, with which they make music on, and named the Kalawao Band. When a Hawaiian National holiday is nigh, the boys pleased to give their honored and respected Reverend Father a rousing surprise serenade of band music and song before the Church bell ring calling the faithfull to the early morning Mass. To the hour the boys turn out with their instruments and station themselves in front of Father Damien's home. The playing of a lively tune on their tin flutes, steel, bones and drums break out on the silent morning air that aroused not only Father Damien but the whole neighborhood of the Kalawao Settlement from their peaceful slumber to hurriedly dress and rushed to the mission ground where the music racket is going on in full blast. Father Damien appeared on the upper verandah of his house and his morning greeting to the boys below: "Poe keiki kolo he." At the sound of his voice, the boys ceased playing on their instruments and the beautiful contralto voice of a leper youth by name Pake the leading soloist of the Church choir ring out like a soaring lark songster on the still morning air of the following Hawaiian composition.

Father Damien is attention during the singing of the song by his boys:

Eia ae a Damiano	Here is Damien
Ka makua a kakou	The father of all of us
He poniponi na maka	Eyes of blue
He alohilohi na aniani	Glasses that sparkle
Ke ike aku oe kau e ka lia	At the sight of him there is such affection

(All the boys join in singing the chorus)

A he ohana like kakou	We are of one family
Na ka makua hookahi no	And of one parent
Goodbye oe goodbye kakou	Good-bye to you, good-bye to us all
A e huli hoi ne me ke aloha	And turn with aloha
Ke hoonani ia ke akua	When blessed by God
Ka makua mana loa	The all-powerful God
Ma na lani kiekie, ae	In the heavens above
Malu ina kanaka ma ka	Sheltering His people
Honua makemake i ka pono	On the earth who yearn for justice

Father Aubert Bouillon—
On approaching St. Philomena's church, I heard singing like that of the Jews weeping on the banks of Babylon over the remembrance of Jerusalem. It was a group of young leper girls singing in their native tongue.

Damien—
At the High Mass on Sunday, my children sing like consummate musicians. Alas! Tuberculosis and death come to take away from me the best voices in my choir.

I found one of my little girls who asked me to bring her Holy Viaticum. When she finished her thanksgiving, she gave up her soul to God. Yesterday, I myself made her coffin and dug her grave.

Charles Warren Stoddard—
There is a small cemetery almost under the eaves of the chapel, where little children are buried—as if they would be lonely out yonder on the plain.

Damien—
I wanted my children with me dead and alive.

Charles Warren Stoddard—
Father Damien knew each individual case; like the good physician that he is, ministering to the bodies as well as to the souls of his flock, his finger is on the pulse of his suffering people, as with painful gravity he watches the tide of life slowly ebbing day by day.

Ambrose Hutchison—
The Hospital was the pivot of Father Damien De Veuster the ministering Angel and Comforter of the sick and dying.

R. W. Meyer—
A great want has been felt by the inmates of the Hospitals for many years; it is simply a little house for the dead to be taken into immediately after death has taken place. Thus far they have been allowed to remain on their beds till burial time to the very great discomfort of the remaining sick.

The hospital compound. Damien was there every day.

The More We Bury the More Are Sent to Us

DAMIEN—
Since I have been here I have buried from one hundred and ninety to two hundred every year, and still the number of living lepers is always over seven hundred.

The more we bury the more are sent to us.

As fast as the old ones die off new ones arrive at the settlement, which thus keeps always full.

CHARLES WARREN STODDARD—
They are all, or nearly all of them, dwelling within sound of the busy hammer that is shaping the coffins which are to enclose their remains! That hammer seemed never idle; coffins were piled where they were visible to all who passed the workshop; and yet two or three per week are called for, and "God's acre" is crowded with the dead.

DAMIEN—
There are many empty places in the church, but in the cemetery there is hardly room left to dig the graves.

Dr. Arthur Mouritz—
His house stood in close proximity and to the LEE side of the burial ground connected with his church, in this said burial ground over 1,000 leper corpses were buried. Owing to the rocky nature of the ground in some places, the corpses were not regularly distributed, in places two, three, four coffins were placed on top of each other.

Damien—
The other day I could not help but be annoyed because someone had started to dig a grave close to the big cross, right at the spot that I had reserved for myself a long time ago!! By insisting, I kept my place vacant. As the cemetery, the church and the presbytery form a single park, I am the sole night-watchman of this fine garden of the dead—all my spiritual children—I find my pleasure in going there to say my rosary and to meditate on the eternal happiness which a great number of them already enjoy, on the eternal unhappiness of some who would not obey me. The cemetery and the dying-ward are my finest books of meditation, both to nourish my own heart and to prepare my instructions.

The Princess Regent Was Deeply Moved

PACIFIC COMMERCIAL ADVERTISER—
The Princess Regent and party landed at about 12:20 p.m. As the boats neared the landing, several of the affectionate and loyal people rushed into the sea and would have carried the boats ashore, but other arrangements having been previously made to facilitate the disembarkation prevented their doing so. On landing, Her Royal Highness was heartily cheered and most enthusiastically received by a large assemblage of the people, both native and foreign. Now it was a genuine greeting commenced, in which nearly all the 800 lepers of the Settlement were there. Some of the poor lepers (about seventy-five), rudely uniformed as soldiers, were drawn up in order as an escort. A temporary wharf had been made; a large lanai, or booth, for reception, and the pathway to it from the beach strewn with evergreens and flowers. Many arches with loyal inscriptions were erected, and a remarkable display made, considering the unhappy state of the people, the short notice of about two days of the expected visit.—and all was devised under the direction of good Father Damien and the Superintendent, Mr. Meyer.

The lepers cheered at first their Alii Makuakane (Princess Mother) as they hailed her, and then sorrow overspread their distorted countenances. The Princess Regent was deeply moved on beholding the effects of the disease on the people, so many of whom she knew personally. She wanted to speak, but her lips only trembled.

Princess Regent Liliʻuokalani visited the settlement in 1881.

I Am Your Friend, Liliuokalani, Regent

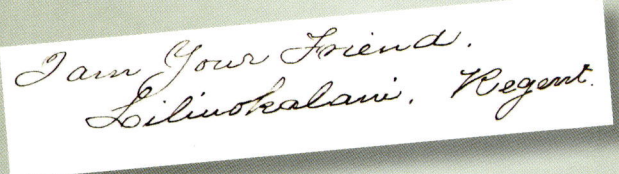

Princess Liliuokalani—
Reverend Sir:
It is my desire to express to you my great appreciation of your heroic and self denying labors, among the most unfortunate of the subjects of this Realm, and in some public manner to testify to the fidelity and patient, loving care with which you labor for the physical and spiritual good of those who are necessarily shut off from the tender ministrations of relatives and friends.

I am aware that your labors and sacrifices are dictated solely by a desire to benefit your unfortunate fellow men and that you look for your reward and inspiration to the divine Father and Ruler of us all–nevertheless, in furtherance of my desire I ask you, Reverend Father, to accept the Order of Knight Commander of the Royal Order of Kalakaua in testimony of my sincere appreciation of your efforts in alleviating the distresses and mitigating in many ways the sorrows of the unfortunate lepers of Kalawao, as I had occasion to observe during my recent visit to that place.

I am your Friend,
Liliuokalani, Regent

The announcement of Damien's decoration with the Royal Order of Kalakaua.

Sir Knight Will Have to Be in the Confessional from Two to Nine o'Clock!

Damien—
I give my word as Knight Commander of the Order of Kalakaua that I will dedicate all my strength for the spiritual and temporal welfare of the unfortunate lepers.

Ambrose Hutchison—
Father Damien's humanity had no use to him of his decoration of honor.

The first and last day Father Damien was seen to sport the brilliant in public.

Damien—
Sir Knight will have to be in the confessional from two to nine o'clock!

The medal he chose not to wear.

I Am Still Almost the Same

Damien—
My health is very good.

Bishop Hermann Koeckemann—
Strong as a Turk.

Damien—
I am still almost the same, except for my beard which is beginning to turn a little grey.

The Queen Seeing with Her Own Eyes

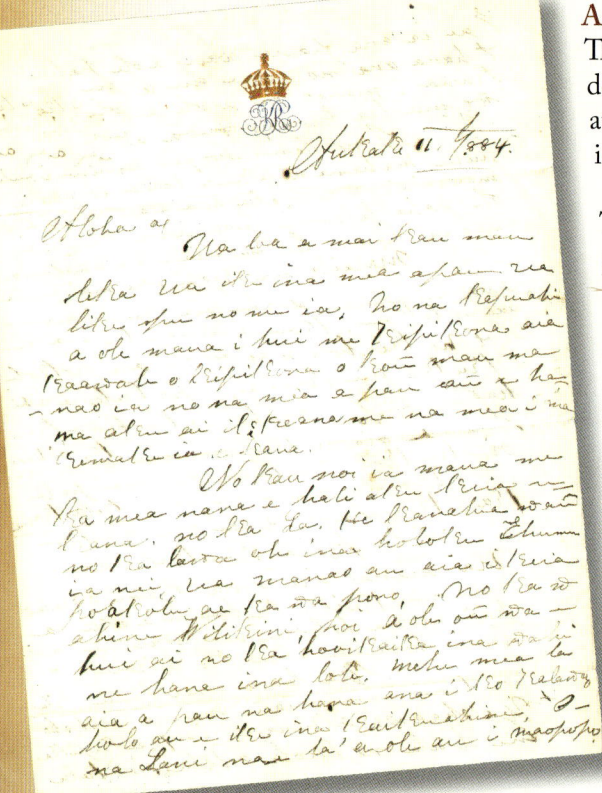

AMBROSE HUTCHISON—
The Queen with her superintendent entered every house and hut at Kalaupapa and Makanalua inhabited by lepers.

The Queen greeted the occupants, "Aloha," as she entered the house or hut and the Queen's greeting returned in kind, "Aloha," with sobs. She would ask the state of their health and how they fared? The replies in general of the stricken people to the Queen's inquiry was "pilikia," the Hawaiian word that means hardship and suffering. The Queen seeing with her own eyes the poverty, squalor and squalid bare conditions of the homes of some of her people, was visibly affected and her only comment heard of the scene she was witnessing was "Kaumaha nohoi!" (deep sorrow).

The Queen went through the entire Hospital buildings, peeks in the dying den and told the name of the shack, she shuddered and expressed her horror in no uncertain terms.

She bore the strain courageously in her determination to see it through.

Queen Kapi'olani corresponded with Damien after her visit to Kalawao in 1884, maintaining an active interest in the welfare of the people of the settlement.

Here I Am, Already 10 Years in the Service of the Plague-Stricken

Kapiolani—
The people here are supporting me in whatever I ask for the lepers of Molokai because of your good and charitable work for our people. Give my best regards to our friends there when you meet them. Who are the patients of the hospital who died recently? Do you want some furniture for the house and plants?

Please be kind enough to give me some news.

Damien—
Here I am, already 10 years in the service of the plague-stricken—without having contracted the disease.

Since coming to the leprosy settlement, I have confided to Our Lord, his Holy Mother, and Saint Joseph the matter of my health. It is up to them to preserve me from this terrible sickness, which they have done so far. And even as for physical things, I often repeat in the midst of the dangers that surround me—"In te Domine speravi non confundar in eternam"—I have put my hope in thee, Lord, and I will not be confounded in eternity. Pau ia—enough of this.

Kapiʻolani and her party at Kalawao.

Life at Kalawao

Damien in the last weeks of his life

Unto Death
1884–1889

J Damien
cath pr. for the lepers.

By 1884, Damien's eleventh year at Kalawao, his twentieth as a priest, the population of the settlement had risen to close to 800, and the graveyard count was more than a thousand. Damien was in his mid-forties, as active and vigorous as ever. But leprosy was in him.

Looking back, he thought he might have contracted the disease during his time in Kohala; it could lie latent for years before symptoms showed. At Kalawao, he had always accepted the possibility—"anticipated from my first arrival into the leper settlement, and voluntarely accepted before hand." Arthur Mouritz was struck by his willingness to go among the sufferers, tending to them without taking any precautions. "Here worked Damien night and day, living and sleeping in this polluted, foetid atmosphere: cheerful, careless, and carefree."

The definitive diagnosis came at the turn of 1884–1885, when he was examined by Mouritz and Dr. Eduard Arning, a German microbiologist hired by the Board of Health to do research and carry out experiments.

The evidence was unmistakable. Damien wrote: "There are signs of it on my left cheek and ear, and my eyebrows are beginning to fall; I shall soon be disfigured."

He had dedicated his life to the people of Kalawao. Now it was certain that he would die among them, of their disease. He took this as a blessing. "People pity me and think me unfortunate, but I think myself the happiest of missionaries. I would not be cured if the price of my cure was that I must leave the Island and give up my work. Since I can always do a little good, I will remain at my post until death."

In the four years that remained to him, he did more than "a little good." Leprosy continued to rage in the Islands, and the numbers at the settlement kept growing, to close to a thousand. The further Damien's illness advanced, the harder he worked. And the more his fame spread.

In 1888, reinforcements finally arrived at the settlement, ending the isolation that had been Damien's torment as a priest. Now there were three other priests, two lay brothers, and three Franciscan sisters. By the end of 1888, Damien's leprosy was entering its last stages. "He has the appearance of a real leper," wrote Father Corneille Limburg, "his face puffed, his ears swollen, his eyes bloodshot, and his voice hoarse. But that doesn't discourage him. He is happy. He works as though he were not sick at all, and he'll stop only when he drops."

The end came on April 15, 1889, four days before Good Friday. Damien spoke from his deathbed: "The Lord is calling me to celebrate Easter with him. I am very satisfied and very happy. I am going gently to my grave."

He was buried where he wanted to lie—under the puhala, the pandanus tree by St. Philomena Church, where he had sheltered in his first days at Kalawao.

Dr. Arthur Mouritz—
He was active and vigorous, of good physique, upright in his carriage, measured 5 feet and 8 inches in height, weighed 204 pounds; his chest was 41 inches in circumference, his hands and feet were shapely, although his fingers were stubbed and callused from toil. His features were regular, his face fleshy, round, and of good dimensions; the color of his eyes brown, his hair black and abundant; his forehead of average breadth and height. He had a clear ringing voice, possessed a powerful barytone, and was a good singer. The view of his full face gave the onlooker the idea of force, harshness and sternness, due in part to the squareness of his chin and lower jaw. His profile was handsome, was softer and more in harmony with the entire cast of his features than the view his full face presented. Having a wealth of hair, he roamed about bareheaded, resulting in his face becoming bronzed by exposure to the wind and sun's rays.

Joseph Dutton—
He had great natural vitality and strength. These powers coupled with his zeal seemed to enable him to be ever ready to pursue with vigor whatever seemed to him ought to be done.

He did not give much time to the study of expediency, of the cost nor the dangers.

The thought of the moment, as things first occurred to him, gave his "cue," and "off he was"—to use one of his very frequent expressions. "Off I am, Brother Joseph," he said to me daily, almost hourly.

Always ready to take up with great vigor anything that presented itself as his actual duty; and further, anything at all that he thought would be good whether it was actually his duty or not.

Full of plans, talking of what he wished for the lepers, the dreams he always had.

Father Damien made no distinction in the bestowal of his favors.

John Puaina Wilmington—
His charity to non-Catholics was just as large as towards his own people.

David Kamahawa—
Gentle and just with everyone.

Pohaku Melemaikea—
Without exception.

Charles Warren Stoddard—
Everywhere he was welcomed as a friend.

Joseph Dutton—
His love for the people of the leper settlement—all of them—was very great. He gave himself for them freely: a sudden call of charity; one in distress, would cause him to drop at once what he might be engaged upon (except when at the altar) and to quickly give his aid. In his ministrations with the natives he was untiring.

Joseph Dutton—
He was very hospitable and made a practice of meeting the weekly steamer at Kalaupapa.

For a long time the steamer arrived very early in the morning, and, in order to reach the landing in time, he used to say his Mass, on those mornings, at about four o'clock, so that he was among the foremost in meeting any passengers.

Dr. Arthur Mouritz—
Both Father Damien and Mr. Ambrose Hutchison had steaming hot coffee and warm food for all who were landed.

Dr. J. H. Stallard—
It was my fortune to see the arrival of a cargo of lepers. They were simply "dumped" upon the shore, and left to "shift" for themselves. Some of the young had happily been provided by the sisters at Kakaako with a letter to Father Damien, soliciting his interest in their welfare but the rest, if not too feeble to walk, were left to shift for themselves.

A steamer from Honolulu at Kalaupapa.

I Will Treat Him and with the Grace of God He May Be Saved

Dr. Arthur Mouritz—
I was at the landing waiting in the lee of the freight house, sheltered from wind and rain, when I was accosted by a diminutive, girlish figure, asking if I was Father Damien, as she carried a letter from the Sisters at Kakaako detention station for him. This little girl, not full ten years old, told a pitiful story—she was soaked to the skin with rain and sea, and shivering with cold, was anxious to get food, shelter and a place to sleep. She was self-possessed, informed me her father had died on the steamer, and was buried at Pukoo, a port on the lee side of Molokai; also on the steamer, too ill to be landed was her little brother 6 years old, who was a leper as well as this little girl herself.

I speedily passed her along to Father Damien and some kokua women who fed and warmed the child and gave her dry clothing.

Damien—
The boat has just arrived and the doctor has examined Makakuka. I am sorry to say he cannot get out as he has the leprosy.

I will treat him and with the grace of God he may be saved.

Do not forget to send him some money.

CHARLES WARREN STODDARD—
He is working with them and for them night and day.

JOSEPH MANU—
He had no fear of the disease.

JOHN PUAINA WILMINGTON—
The boys dormitories were right up against Father Damien's house, the windows and doors of his house were open. During the night the lights were always on.

JOSEPH MANU—
He worked with the children and took no precautions.

He wanted to be their father.

CHARLES WARREN STODDARD—
His intimates are lepers; his house is hardly ever free from them.

Dr. Arthur Mouritz—
In the kindness of his nature, he never forbade lepers entering his house; they had access to it any time, night or day. I named his house "Kalawao Family House and Lepers' Rest," free beds, free board for the needy; this designation I believe could not be improved upon, it exactly fitted the prevailing conditions.

Charles Warren Stoddard—
It is true that he does his own cooking and his own housework, and whatever is to be done about the altar; a native, not a leper, washes for him, and mends his clothing when necessary; but the tools that are so often in his hands are handled by lepers; and whatever is passed about the village comes to him from those who are, to put it broadly, in all stages of decomposition.

G. W. Woods—
The pipe was filled and passed to him, although but just removed from a leper's mouth; he ate poi out of the family calabash; he fondled the children, and dressed the wounds of all who needed this attention, evidently to secure the confidence and love of these people whom he had adopted in his heart, that he might bring them to Christ.

Dr. Arthur Mouritz—
Here worked Damien night and day, living and sleeping in this polluted, foetid atmosphere: cheerful, careless, and carefree.

Dr. Arthur Mouritz—

The first meeting I had with Fr. Damien the dark copper color of the skin of his forehead attracted my attention, it was the visible proof of the invasion of the Destroyer.

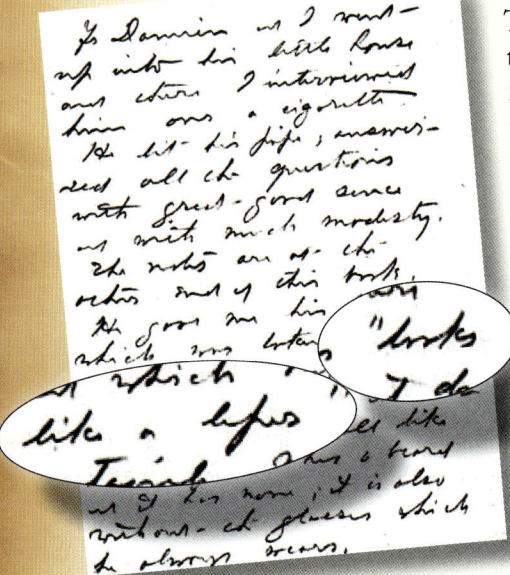

Charles Warren Stoddard—

He gave me his photograph, which was taken here and which he says "looks like a leper," and so it does.

Ambrose Hutchison—

Father Damien going to Honolulu was the annual retreat of the Fathers and Mission business. Father Damien returned to the leper settlement. In the first boat that came into the crevice of the rock was Father Damien who step ashore from the boat. He had his left foot bandaged. Mutual greeting passed between us. Naturally I asked the Father how he hurt his foot? Came the prompt answer, "I did it with hot water." "Hot water?" I said surprised. Yes, while at the mission, I had taken a bath and poured some hot water in it to wash my feet, I put my foot into the water, I did not feel the heat and I did not know it was too hot. The result is as you see, I blistered my foot and added calling me by my name with a touch of irony, "I think I have the disease," and limped away.

A page from the diary of Charles Warren Stoddard, visiting Damien at the settlement.

I Made these Notes from His Own Lips

Joseph Dutton—
I made these notes from his own lips, using as near as I could his very words, and read the statement all over to him before he signed it.

Served as priest on the Island of Hawaii, from 1864 to 1873. Occasionally, heard confessions of lepers; ministered to them in their cabins sometimes, but had no constant or very particular contact with them, until he came here to the leper settlement, in 1873; since which time, his contact and association, have been almost constant. In 1873, was strong and healthy, with remarkably robust constitution. Has never had any sexual intercourse whatever. Am quite sure, that when near to lepers, as at confession, or in their cabins, before coming to the leper settlement; he felt, on each occasion, a peculiar sensation in the face; a sort of itching or burning, and that he felt the same here, at the settlement, during the first two or three years: that he also felt it on the legs.

Am confident that the germs were in his system, certainly within the first three years of his residence here.

His Name Was Duly Recorded on the Official Records

Ambrose Hutchison—
On the 30th day of March A.D. 1886 his name was duly recorded on the Official records: a leper by pronouncement of the resident physician of the Leper Settlement of Kalawao.

Damien's name is entered on the official Board of Health register, number 2886, March 30, 1886.

Leprosy Has Attacked Me

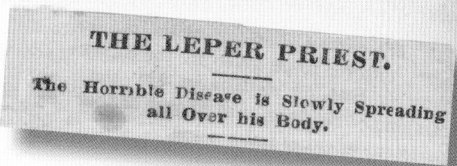

DAMIEN—
Leprosy has attacked me.

The natural consequence of a long stay with these lepers.

Anticipated from my first arrival into the leper asylum, and voluntarely accepted before hand.

It is the memory of having lain beneath the mortuary drape twenty-five years ago—the day of my vows—that led me to brave the dangers of contracting this terrible disease in doing my duty here.

My robust constitution resisted it for a long time. It has been undermined.

There are signs of it on my left cheek and ear, and my eyebrows are beginning to fall; I shall soon be disfigured.

Our Lord has willed stigmatization.

Blessed be God!

Pray for me and us lepers.

As I have no doubt of the real character of the malady, I remain calm, resigned, and very happy in the midst of my people. The good God knows what is best for my sanctification, and I say daily, Fiat voluntas tua, with a ready heart.

I will keep on working as usual.

News of Damien's affliction spreads around the world.

DAMIEN—
I am in charge of two orphanages.

This little world fills my chapel morning and evening and in the day for catechism.

AKANOKI A. WILLS—
Dear Rev. Father Damien:
I suppose you still remember me Akanoki A. Wills of Kaupo. My son Helekia Wills is either at Kalawao or Kalaupapa.

I would like very much if you ask him to stay with you and be your altar boy.

He is growing up to be a man and at the same time the leprosy in him is growing worse.

Give our love to my son and all our friends there.

S. H. MOOKAPU—
Dear Beloved Rev. Father J. Damien:
We are very happy to know that you are taking good care of our boys.

We shall continue to place our trust in you, Father J. Damien. It is true that they are big boys but they should obey you at all times. Teaching them to work with hands, we believe, is right and proper.

Please Reply as This Is an Important Matter

J. W. KELIIKEA—
Dear Father:
Is it true that Tom Makanoanoa is still there?

He and his mother Nohe Makanoanoa were taken from Kona to Molokai. We heard the rumor that he is dead.

We trust you and we know that you will tell us the truth about him.

Please reply as this is an important matter.

CECELIA HALIIMAILE—
Rev. Father Damien:
I am asking you if my daughter Cecelia is at Kalawao or Kalaupapa? If you see her, I would like that you see she is taken good care and also let us know of anything she needs.

Francisco Camacho—
Dear Father:
I send this short note to you because we sent some Christmas presents to our child Peter Camacho to be under your care and that you will open the box yourself and give it to him whatever it contains. Such tin of cracker and some toys for him to play with to amuse himself and that I say that should the box be opened by someone else without your knowledge everything will be lose before you know of as it happens in many instances.

Well Father we send our greetings to you and to our child Peter, our beloved child, and tell him he should not forget to pray to God, Our Father and Our Lord Jesus Christ and that he must obey you in all things whatever you command him to do right for that is I always wish for him to do.

Dear Father Damien I was very glad when I heard that my child was in your hand and that he was doing very well—under your management. Dear Father, I am very grateful to you for the care of my child in the strange land without any hope for our seeing him again in this world so Father good-bye for the present and tell Peter that we all send our love and greetings to him from his brothers and sisters tell him that they never did forget him for a moment from the day he left Honolulu till this moment and that he ought to be very thankful for following with such a good kind Father as you to be under the heaven.

So good-bye once more Father and God bless you with my child in your place of retreat ever and ever yours.

Damien—
On Sunday I usually celebrate a Mass. I preach four times, and give communion twice.

Christmas Eve—I take my therapeutic bath at five in the morning; at six I leave for Kalaupapa. I say Mass, preach, then hear confessions until 11:30, still fasting.

I come back to Kalawao, eat, then go into the confessional and stay there until seven.

I say my breviary. I drink a cup of coffee and go back to the church at nine where the children and young people are waiting for the general examination of the catechism; that lasts until 11:30.

At midnight, High Mass begins and I preach for over half an hour.

Four o'clock in the morning, I return to Kalaupapa to sing a second Mass and preach another sermon. After that I give solemn Baptism to several catechumens.

At nine o'clock I say the third Mass at Kalawao, but this time I'm worn out and one of my good catechists preaches the sermon.

After this I think about getting Christmas dinner.

Mary Kikila—

Dear Damien:
Will you be kind enough to send Keaka Lui to go and put the graves of David Malo and Hana in good shape?

I was told these graves need repair.

Damien—

I am a cripple, probably for life. I walk but drag my leg to come and go to the hospital, which is not even 5 minutes from here. It's a fatigue that makes me cry all through the night.

I usually go from one church to another in a carriage.

Dr. Arthur Mouritz—

He lost at least thirty-five pounds in bodily weight at this time. He tottered in his walk, his clothes appeared like bags hung on his figure.

Father Damien, "Kamiano," continues to be called upon to attend to the needs of his people.

I Have Never Been So Isolated

Damien—
My disease is progressing, and my face and hands are undergoing a transformation.

Do not pity me too much.

As my disease advances, I am more and more blessed.

I ask but one favor: send to me in this tomb someone who can be my confessor.

I have never been so isolated and excluded from all communication with my confreres.

Being without a good confessor is more difficult to bear than all the rest.

I resign myself to Divine Providence, and find my consolation in the only companion who does not leave me—that is to say, our Divine Savior in the Holy Eucharist—it is at the foot of the altar that I often confess myself and seek relief from spiritual pain.

—Josephus Damianus De Veuster, leprous sinner who confesses so rarely

Bishop Hermann Koeckemann—
Know that your loneliness troubles me very much, but what can I do?

Alas, I Am Not Worthy

Damien—
Before Him and before the statue of our Holy Mother, I sometimes whisper, asking for the conservation of my health.

I still await our Lord through the intercession of our good Mother to perform a miracle in my favor, but alas, I am not worthy.

Dr. Arthur Mourtiz—
"Melancholia Religiosa," strange to say, occasionally troubled him– THE DELUSION OF HIS BEING UNWORTHY OF HEAVEN. This was most remarkable, for if there was any man in the universe who had every prospect of future happiness and salvation, that man was Damien.

Damien—
You know, the pastor of Kalawao has not yet been confirmed in grace notwithstanding the pompous titles conferred on him.

Dr. Arthur Mourtiz—
Years of privation, hardship and disagreeable work, nights of watching and answering calls to the sick and dying at all hours, vigils and many weary hours passed in the night and darkness by the bleak and inhospitable shores of Kalaupapa, awaiting the homeless leper and ORPHAN—all this work must count, and it is amply sufficient to win salvation for Damien.

W. H. Kahumoku—
Dear Father:
I still love and esteem you as Father and a true friend and keeper of our Agnes who is still at the settlement.

May God bless you in your noble work for Christ and His followers.

Christina is just crying her heart for you.

Damien—
People pity me and think me unfortunate, but I think myself the happiest of missionaries.

I would not be cured if the price of my cure was that I must leave the Island and give up my work.

What would become of my poor sufferers? No! Since I can always do a little good, I will remain at my post until death.

Damien—
When will the hospital sisters arrive?

Sister Leopoldina Burns—
I knew I could not last long he said and many years I have been begging our Dear Lord to send someone to fill my place.

—And now see how He has answered my prayer. 'prase glory, and thanks be to our great and Mighty God."

Joseph Dutton—
Mother Marianne, the Franciscan Sister from Syracuse, New York, is in charge of the Girls' Home at Kalaupapa. She has four other sisters with her.

Father Leonor Fouesnel—
These excellent daughters of St. Francis knew in advance what kind of occupation they would have.

One Could Never Imagine What a Lonely Barren Place It Was

Sister Leopoldina Burns—
Our little steamer was rolling and plowing through the raging waves.

The lepers were put in the cattle's place with no shelter and no bed poor creatures if they were sick and there was not as much attention paid to them as there would be to the sick cattle.

When the ship cast anchor the ocean was as smoothe as a river bed, we went down the rope ladder just at day brake, and our little boat glided over the smooth surface of the ocean as if it was glad to cast us into the valley of death.

One could never imagine what a lonely barren place it was. Not a tree or a shrub in the whole Settlement only in the church yard where there were a few poor little trees that were so bent and yellow by the continued sweep of the birning wind it would make one sad to look at them.

A painting of the settlement in late 1888.

DAMIEN—
How good God is to have preserved me long enough to have the good Sisters of Charity at the leproserie.

FATHER CORNEILLE LIMBURG—
He seemed to revive and forget all suffering and illness for joy at the arrival of the sisters.

SISTER LEOPOLDINA BURNS—
How thin and sick he looked his face so ashy and yet he was cheerful and happy.

MOTHER MARIANNE COPE—
Father Damien conducted us to the orphanage of the leprous girls at Kalawao. "My children," he told them, "I shall die soon but you will not be abandoned. The Sisters whom you see have come to care for you."

He took us also to visit the boys' orphanage and he showed us how to make their garments. At a later visit, he asked us, suddenly, "Will you take care of my boys when I am gone?" Three times he repeated the question. We promised him.

SISTER LEOPOLDINA BURNS—
He stretched his poor disfigured hands to heaven thanking our Divine Lord that help had come.

Mother Marianne Cope of the Franciscan Sisters, who came to the settlement in 1888.

A Hundred Orphans who Are under My Charge

Damien—
I have two priests by my side.

Besides these I have with me two Brothers, who help me with the care of a hundred orphans who are under my charge.

Damien with boys of Kalawao, in the final weeks of his life (top photo). Damien continues to provide for his orphans to the last (bottom photos).

Edward Clifford—
Two earnest laymen—Brother Joseph, an American, and Brother James.

Sister Leopoldina Burns—
Brother James had charge of the small boys.

Damien—
Mr. Dutton is truly an example of a self-devoting man and as he has a good will I very soon will have him initiated for any kind of service what may be expected from him.

Ambrose Hutchison—
Mr. Dutton went to work with a will and became an adept washer and dresser of sores that relieved Father Damien of the work.

Joseph Dutton—
I have had a busy day, have dressed nearly two hundred sores, some of the lepers waiting their turn in line for four or five hours.

Damien—
He is of exemplary conduct and truly pious.

He's truly a good confrere to me.

I have built him a little hermitage near the pu hala tree.

Damien—
I am happy and content and fairly strong, even if very disfigured.

Joseph Dutton—
One of his ears is swollen to an enormous size and covered with lumps of many colors; on his forehead ridges and lumps, also on the face and arms. Yet he is very active and cheerful, one of the most powerful men physically to be found.

Damien—
Fortunately my hands, though quite sore, are not yet crippled.

We have finished building a second large dormitory for our orphans.

As my faithful here are always on the increase, I am obliged to enlarge my church considerably.

Dr. Arthur Mouritz—
He even appeared to me to work harder as his strength gradually became sapped by the disease.

David Ilihia—
He never lost courage.

He Strained Every Nerve and Muscle

Joseph Dutton—
When he felt that his end was approaching, and having quite a number of pieces of unfinished work on hand—about the new church, etc.—he strained every nerve and muscle to get them completed.

David Ilihia—
I saw him build the church. Prepare the lime, saw wood—he worked as an ordinary worker.

The interior of St. Philomena Church as Damien would have last seen it (top photo). Damien the tireless builder—hammer and nails to the last (bottom photo).

Sister Leopoldina Burns—
His Priestly hands were grayish purple and badly swollen the joints of those anointed fingers twice their natural size and some of them with ulcers.

Joseph Sinnett—
I have seen him under a tropical sun, covered with sweat and dust, sawing and hammering away with his lepers.

Sister Leopoldina Burns—
His cassock was badly soiled with lime, cement, and paint.

Father Corneille Limburg—
To my utter amazement, I saw him on his church which he was roofing, giving orders to masons, workers and carpenters. And yet he has the appearance of a real leper, his face puffed, his ears swollen, his eyes bloodshot, and his voice hoarse. But that doesn't discourage him. He is happy. He works as though he were not sick at all, and he'll stop only when he drops.

Sister Leopoldina Burns—
He was so overjoyed about his new church and to think he had been able to finish it.

How happy he was! his manner was like a child who had received a great gift.

His kind Saintly face was glowing with delight.

He Gives Himself No Airs of Martyr, Saint, or Hero

EDWARD CLIFFORD—
He is now forty-nine years old—a thick-set, strongly-built man, with black curly hair and short beard, turning gray. His countenance must have been handsome, with a full, well-curved mouth and a short, straight nose; but he is now a good deal disfigured with leprosy, though not so badly as to make it anything but a pleasure to look at his bright, sensible face. His forehead is swollen and ridged, the eyebrows are gone, the nose is somewhat sunk, and the ears are greatly enlarged. His hands and face look uneven with a sort of incipient boils, and his body also shows many signs of the disease.

He gives himself no airs of martyr, saint, or hero—a humbler man I never saw.

He seldom talked of himself except in answer to questions, and he had always about him the simplicity of a great man—"clothed with humility."

Damien sketched (above) and painted (opposite) by Edward Clifford.

I Did Not Know the Disease Had Made Such Progress

He was not a sentimental kind of man, and I was therefore the more pleased that he gave me a little card of flowers from Jerusalem, and wrote on it, "To Edward Clifford, from his leper friend, J. Damien." He also wrote in my Bible the words, "I was sick, and ye visited me."

Some of my happiest times at Molokai were spent sketching him and listening to what he said.

The lepers often came up to watch my progress.

There were generally several of them playing in the garden below us.

It was pleasant to see how happy and at home they were. Their poor faces were often swelled and drawn and distorted, with bloodshot goggle eyes; but I felt less horror than I expected at their strange aspect.

He looked mournfully at my work. "What an ugly face!" he said; "I did not know the disease had made such progress."

Joseph Dutton—
Father Damien is suffering very much now, though he is out and about every day. He says Mass every day, has missed only two mornings since I came here and these on account of his eyes.

Damien—
Today a small inflammation in my eyes has stopped me, for the first time, from celebrating Holy mass and if it doesn't improve in one or two hours, I'll have to stop praying the breviary for the first time since 1864.

I am getting old and weak. I know that my days are numbered, and do not expect to be in this miserable world for long.

I am persuaded that the will of the Lord is that I die in the same way and of the same sickness as my afflicted sheep.

The work of the lepers is assured. I am no longer necessary, and so will go up yonder.

Father Wendelin Moellers—
From March 28 on he did not leave his room.

That day he arranged his temporal affairs.

Damien's Will

LAST WILL AND TESTAMENT—
I J. Damien De Veuster catholic priest a resident of the leper Asylum at Molokai being of sound mind and memory do make publish and declare this my last will and testament.

I give and bequeath all of my estate real personal and mixed which I may possess in the Hawaiian Islands at the time of my Death, unto the Right Reverend Hermann Koeckemann Bishop of Alba and Vicar Apostolic of the Hawaiian Islands, and to his Successor in office.

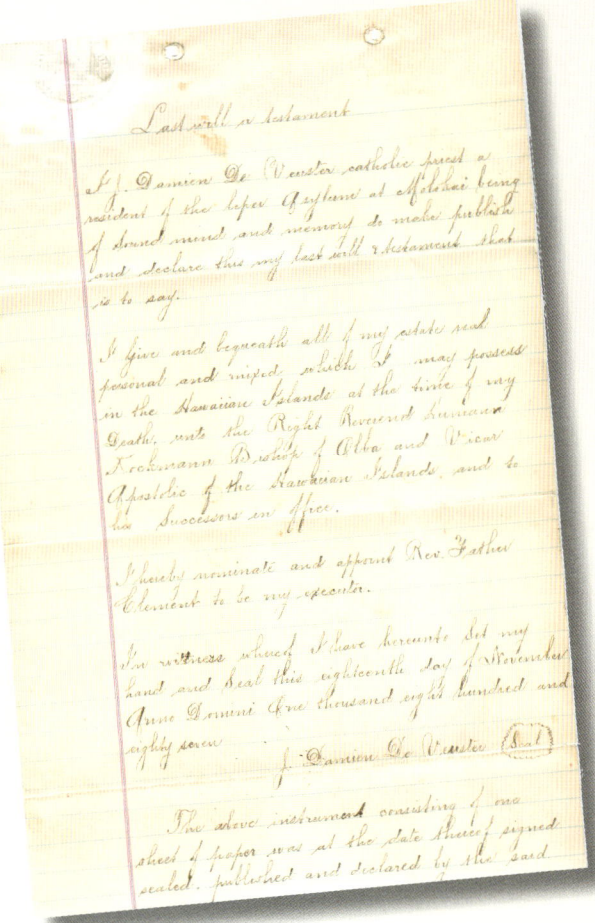

Damien's will—"Now I die poor."

Damien—
Now I die poor; I have nothing of my own.

Father Louis-Lambert Conrardy—
The poor Father suffers a great deal. He is all disfigured; his voice is almost gone. If you could see him as I do, in his little room, lying on his bed on the floor, tears would come to your eyes.

Father Wendelin Moellers—
What I most admired in him was his admirable patience. He was so ardent, so active, so robust, to be nailed down to his miserable bed.

He was laid on the ground on a wretched mattress, like the poorest leper, and we had great difficulty in making him accept a bed. And how poorly off he was! He who had spent so much money in relieving the lepers, had forgotten himself so far as not to have even a change of linen, or sheets for his bed.

Damien's eyeglasses and walking stick, his rosary, and one of his devotional books.

The Day Before His Death

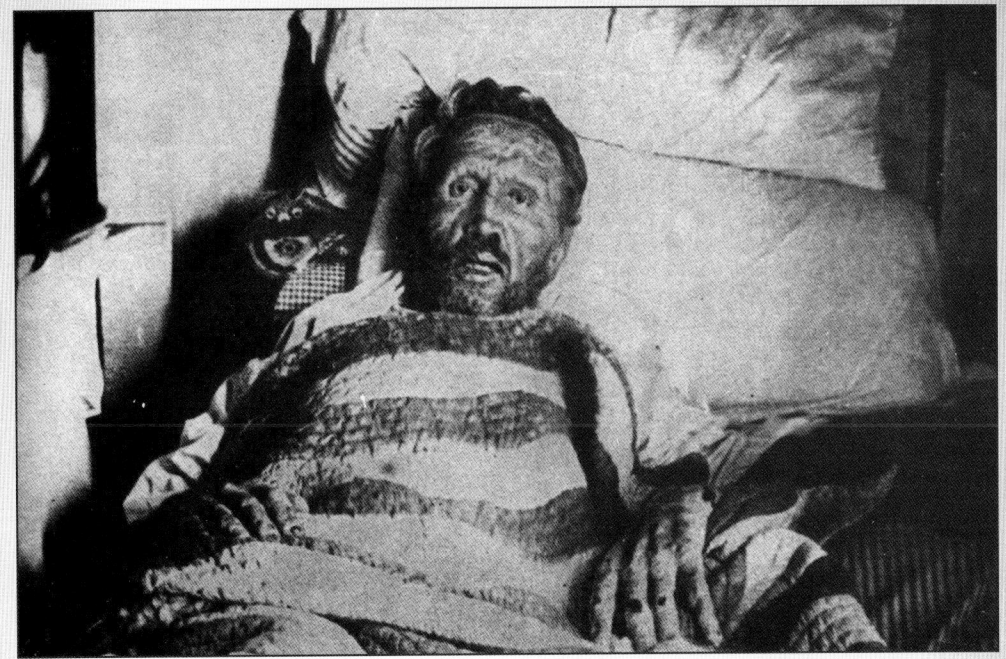

Joseph Dutton—
The day before his death, I raised him up in his bed for the government physician to get a photograph. It is the most striking picture I have seen of him.

Damien—
Very soon I hope all will be right—when the body is under the green coverlet.

R. W. Meyer—
They are digging & preparing poor father Damien's grave.

On his deathbed, the day before he died.

Damien—
The Lord is calling me to celebrate Easter with Him.

I am very satisfied and very happy.

I am going gently to my grave.

Father Wendelin Moellers—
He died quietly as if asleep.

The good shepherd had given his life for his sheep.

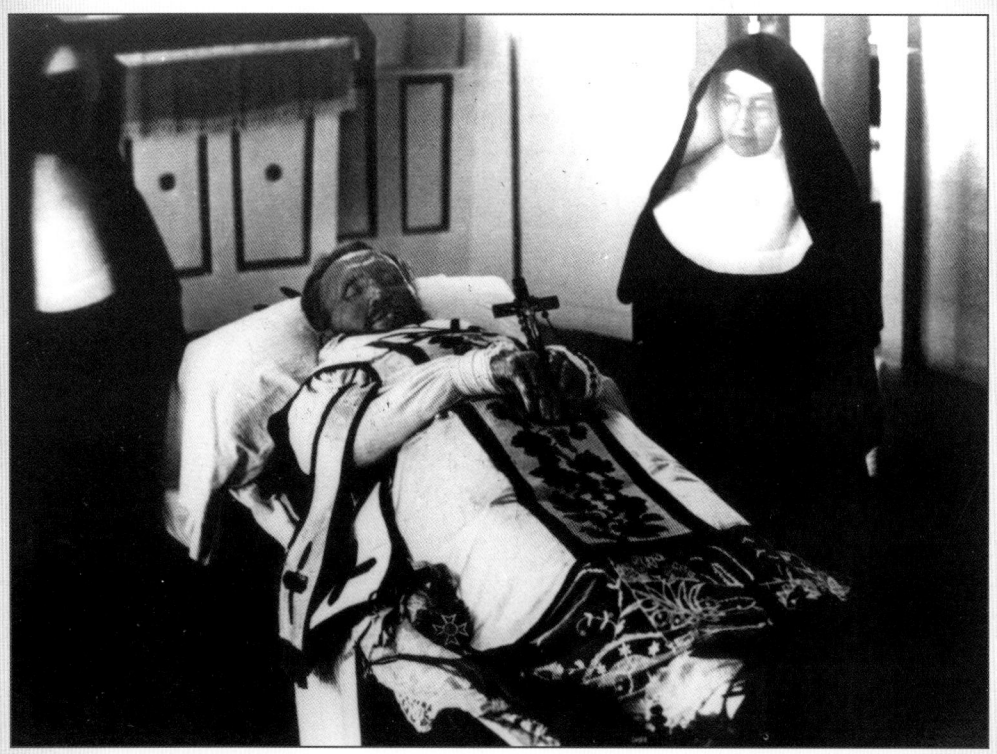

Robed for his last Mass; with Mother Marianne and Sister Leopoldina.

A Rough Board Box in the Shape of a Coffin

FATHER WENDELIN MOELLERS—
The good Sisters came to decorate his coffin.

SISTER LEOPOLDINA BURNS—
The poor little cart and old black horse were sent for us, and again Mother and I moved slowly over that lonely road, the dark clouds covered the sun while the weard sad cry of the wind as it swept over the dark gray rocks that seemed to frown down on us from there lofty place on the side of the great mountain. When we reached the home there was a dead silence everywhere the poor boys were in little groups, like sheep without their shepherd.

Father Conrardy led us to a clean place in the yard where they had put on two benches a rough board box in the shape of a coffin.

We went to work, and the skillful hands of our Mother transformed that ugly rough box in to a beautiful casket.

FATHER WENDELIN MOELLERS—
They lined the inside with white silk, and covered the outside with black cloth, on which was a white cross.

SISTER LEOPOLDINA BURNS—
Then the Fathers after dressing the remains of the Saintly Priest in his beautiful white vestments placed him in his pretty casket and carried him in his new church.

The Men Lepers Carried the Remains to the Grave

Pohaku Melemaikea—
Everyone from Kalawao and Kalaupapa went to the funeral.

Sister Mary Vincentia Mccormick—
After the Mass the men lepers carried the remains to the grave.

This was the saddest procession I have ever seen, the lame leaning upon their sticks, the blind led by others, the deformed,—all joined the ranks.

Brother James Sinnett—
We laid him to rest under his puhalla-tree.

Damien's funeral—"the saddest procession I have ever seen."

Sister Mary Vincentia McCormick—
The Hawaiian flag was at "half mast" in the settlement.

The musicians put aside their musical instruments and the large Hawaiian flag they carried and climbed up into the tree above the spot where he was buried.

It was sad to see the children near his grave. The smallest boys circled around his grave, then the next size behind them and the taller ones in back of them forming three or four rows. The small children watching their dear Spiritual Father as he was lowered into his grave and their sad little faces looked as though they had lost their best friend.

Joseph Dutton—
Good Father Damien. May he rest in peace.

Damien's grave, by St. Philomena Church.

A statue of the new saint at the De Veuster family home in Tremelo, now a museum.

The Making of a Saint
1889-2009

At Kalawao, Damien had a single aim: to do God's work—to imitate Christ. This did not shield him from controversy, in life or in death. His superiors in the Sacred Hearts mission, Bishop Hermann Koeckemann and Father Leonor Fouesnel, never found him easy to deal with, and once he was gone they could not bring themselves to think of him as a saint. So they were by no means energetic about forwarding the cause—and after all, there was no evidence that Damien had worked miracles at the settlement.

Worse, there was a scandal that attached itself to Damien's name. Soon after he died, a Protestant minister at Honolulu wrote a letter that found its way into print. It accused Damien of sexual immorality, saying that his leprosy came from sleeping with Hawaiian women.

This was the worst kind of slander, entirely without any factual basis, but the letter was reprinted all around the world.

It came to the attention of Robert Louis Stevenson, the most famous author of his time. It so happened that Stevenson, traveling the Pacific, had visited Kalawao just a few weeks after Damien died. He took up his pen and wrote a blistering rebuttal—which also went all round the world.

All this made any kind of calm considered evaluation of Damien impossible.

Then, within a few years, came the cure of Sister Simplicia Hue. But that did not trigger an immediate investigation of Damien's possible sanctity. The Sacred Hearts, a relatively small and relatively new order, had no saints, and there was a school of thought that the first saint should be the founder of the congregation.

There matters rested until the 1930s, when the case of Sister Simplicia began to be seriously considered.

In 1936, Damien's remains were exhumed and returned to his homeland, Belgium, where they were received with acclaim and reinterred in a church crypt in Louvain, the city where he had joined the Sacred Hearts.

It took another two decades, until the mid-fifties, before the cause for the beatification of Damien was introduced, and another four decades, until 1995, before he was beatified by Pope John Paul II in a ceremony in Brussels.

A second miracle was in the making, and it had profound connections with Damien's work. Audrey Toguchi's Hawaiian family had leprosy in its history. Her grandfather had been shipped to Kalawao—wrongly diagnosed, as it turned out—and two of her other relatives, correctly diagnosed, ended their days there. In 1936, Audrey herself, as a young schoolgirl, had watched the procession that carried Damien's remains through the streets of Honolulu to the ship that was to take them on the first leg of the journey back to Belgium. In the 1990s, she was diagnosed with an incurable cancer. She decided to refuse treatment, putting her faith entirely in Damien. "I said to myself, Dear Lord, look at the lady who touched Jesus's hem, she got healed, and he turned around and said your faith has healed you. So who could help me better than the man who loved the local people."

She went to pray at Damien's gravesite, and was healed. Her case was written up in a professional medical journal by the doctor who had treated her. The report made its way to Rome, and this was the beginning of serious investigation of a possible second miracle.

The case survived the necessary rigorous testing, medical and theological. The miracle was formally recognized in 2008, and in 2009, in a ceremony at St. Peter's in Rome, attended by pilgrims from Hawai'i, including residents of Kalaupapa in wheelchairs, Pope Benedict XVI canonized Damien.

Father Damien was now, and would be forever, Saint Damien.

I Felt Great Affection for Him Because of His Charity

Pohaku Melemaikea—
I loved him like a father.

Joseph Manu—
My spiritual father and my friend.

Ambrose Hutchison—
Father Damien was a man of deep faith. He believed in the goodness and love of Almighty God.

Joseph Dutton—
Very devout.

David Kamahawa—
I felt great affection for him because of his charity.

Sister Leopoldina Burns—
His only desire was to love and help the poor lepers.

He would give all he had to the needy even if he himself had to suffer thereby, neither did he expect thanks for his help.

Hadrianus Keoho—
He had few possessions. He practiced poverty.

Mother Judith Brassier—
He went along, indifferent to the rich or poor.

He talked to everybody without any ceremonies.

Edward Clifford—
All who knew him personally must have been struck with the absence of "godliness" in so good a man.

No airs of martyr, saint or hero.

Just a hard-working, simple-minded, unself-conscious man, who thought little about himself, but continually about his business.

Sister Leopoldina Burns—
He forgot himself for his neighbor.

Robert Louis Stevenson—
This plain, noble human brother and father of ours; his imperfections are the traits of his face, by which we know him for our fellow; his martyrdom and his example nothing can lessen or annul.

Joseph Manu—
He really was a saint.

Audrey Toguchi—
When they exhumed his body, I was attending St. Augustine School in the second grade.

All of the school children were taken to Our Lady of Peace Cathedral to attend Father Damien's farewell mass.

Many tears were shed when the requiem mass concluded. The coffin came down the aisle and onto Fort Street.

We assembled with other school students along both-side sidewalks and watched the procession travel to the waiting ship at the wharf. It was a very sorrowful and memorable experience.

Damien's remains are carried in procession through the streets of Honolulu.

The Journey to Belgium

Damien's remains depart from Honolulu (top photo), and arrive in Belgium (bottom photo).

DAVID KAMAHANA—
I felt great pain when the authorities took the remains.

PRESIDENT FRANKLIN DELANO ROOSEVELT—
The recent event of the return of his body to Belgium must freshen in our minds with deep veneration the remembrance of this priest who gave his all for his brother man.

Damien's crypt in St. Anthony's church in Louvain.

Mohandas Gandhi—

The political and journalistic world can boast of very few heroes who compare with Father Damien of Molokai. The Catholic Church, on the contrary, counts by the thousands those who, after the example of Father Damien, have devoted themselves to the victims of leprosy. It is worthwhile to look for the sources of such heroism.

Mother Teresa —

We work among thousands of lepers in India, Yemen, Ethiopia and Tanzania. We set up mobile hospitals and rehabilitation centers on government land. In order to continue this beautiful work of love and healing, we need a saint to lead and protect us. Fr Damien can be this saint. Holy Father, our lepers and everyone on earth beg you to give us a saint, a martyr to love, an example of obedience to our religion.

Mother Teresa at the beatification ceremony in 1995.

HAWAII CATHOLIC HERALD—
The cure happened in 1895 to a 37-year-old French Sacred Hearts Sister named Sister Simplicia Hue. She became ill in February of that year with an influenza-like illness which soon escalated into a severe and painful gastrointestinal disorder. Her condition deteriorated to the point where she suffered a discharge of bloody matter and could not eat. Bronchitis set in and by April she received Holy Viaticum and anointing facing the fact that she would soon die.

At this point, she began a daily novena asking Father Damien to intercede with the invocation: "Father Damien pray for us and cure me." Next to her death bed was Damien's picture. On the evening of Sepember 11, worn out by pain, hunger, fever, and fatigue she lost consciousness. On September 12 at 1:30 a.m. she awoke startled to find herself free of pain. Knowing she had been miraculously cured, she immediately cried out to the infirmarian, "Sister, I'm cured!" Sister Simplicia lived another 32 years until her death in 1927 without any recurrence of this illness.

Pope John Paul II—
I am very happy to welcome the delegates from the Hawaiian Islands:

Walena aloha okou. Ma kakou pakahe a pau ka maluhia a ma ka aloha o Iesu Christo! To all of you, my warmest and most sincere wishes. May the peace and love of Christ be with you!

Blessed Damien, you allowed yourself to be led by the Holy Spirit, as a son obedient to the will of the Father. By your life and by your missionary work, you demonstrate the tenderness and the mercy of Christ for each human being, revealing to him the beauty of his inner being, which no disease, no deformity, no weakness can totally disfigure.

My heart turns to those who today are still suffering from leprosy. In Damien they now have an intercessor, because, before contracting the disease, he had already identified with them and often said: "We others, the lepers."

Fr. Damien displayed a particular form of holiness in his ministry; he was at once a priest, religious and missionary. With these three qualities, he revealed the face of Christ, showing the path of salvation, teaching the Gospel and working tirelessly for development. He organized religious, social and fraternal life on Molokai, at the time an island of banishment from society; with him everyone had a place, each one was recognized and loved by his brothers and sisters.

To confirm to the end the truth of his witness, he offered his life in their midst. He became a leper in the midst of other lepers, he became a leper for the lepers. He suffered and he died like them, believing in the resurrection of Christ, because Christ is the Lord!

Today, through me, the Church acknowledges and confirms the value of Fr. Damien's example along the path of holiness, praising God for having guided him to the end of his life on an often difficult journey.

Audrey Toguchi—
In the days when the leprosy became epidemic, somebody just grabbed my grandfather off Fort Street. He was delivering beverages. They just grab him off Fort Street, marched him right down to the pier. And they decided to put him in the community hospital, for lepers. He was so bent out of shape. Can you imagine a tall haole guy, he's not going to be confined there because he has a family. So what he did in the night time, he climb over the fence and took off home and told my grandmother what happened to him. Well they nabbed him and for his punishment they shipped him to Kalawao, Kalaupapa. The time of Mother Marianne and Brother Joseph Dutton. And he got to say, how he, Father Damien, died with all the locals.

In two years they decided he didn't have leprosy and so he was one of two people who would return to civilization.

Now that is the connection to Father Damien, but later on the two youngest of my father's siblings, my uncle and auntie, both high school students, were seized and taken to Kalihi Hospital. Later they were sent to Kalaupapa and they died over there.

I discovered this information as an adult. This episode was kept in the family as hidden agenda. Only in school did we hear about the horrors of Kalaupapa.

Opposite: A Hawaiian dance of devotion to Damien during the beatification observances.

AUDREY TOGUCHI—
In 1997 my two sisters chose to accompany me to mass at St Philomena Church in Kalawao, Molokai and to pray for an intercession at Father Damien's grave site.

At that time we were praying for a healing of my heart problems.

In 1998, we learned that both of my lungs had been invaded by a very vicious, rare, aggressive, terminal cancer.

I turned completely and solely to Father Damien for a miraculous cure.

I said to myself, Dear Lord, look at the lady who touched Jesus's hem, she got healed, and he turned around and said your faith has healed you. So who could help me better than the man that loved the local people.

Father Damien is the one I asked and I do talk to him like he's my friend.

We continued with our novenas. In the ensuing months, x-rays indicated that the cancers were shrinking. After about five months, they were gone. This was without chemotherapy.

DR. WALTER CHANG—
Histologically proven lung metastases disappeared with no therapy at all.

The evidence for spontaneous regression in this case is convincing.

Pope Benedict XVI—
Jozef De Veuster received the name of Damien in the Congregation of the Sacred Hearts of Jesus and Mary. When he was 23 years old, in 1863, he left Flanders, the land of his birth, to proclaim the Gospel on the other side of the world in the Hawaiian Islands. His missionary activity, which gave him such joy, reached its peak in charity. Not without fear and repugnance, he chose to go to the Island of Molokai to serve the lepers who lived there, abandoned by all. Thus he was exposed to the disease from which they suffered.
He felt at home with them. The servant of the Word consequently became a suffering servant, a leper with the lepers, for the last four years of his life.

President Barack Obama—
Father Damien challenged the stigmatizing effects of the disease, giving voice to the voiceless and ultimately sacrificing his own life to bring dignity to so many.

The Day of Canonization

The day of canonization, October 11, 2009.

Audrey Toguchi—
He brought love and dignity to the forsaken.

Pope Benedict XVI—
Therefore as the Word of Jesus proclaimed to us in today's Gospel says, he received eternal life.

In St. Peter's Basilica (top photo). St. Peter's Square (bottom photo).

Audrey Toguchi with Pope Benedict XVI (top photo).
People of Kalaupapa see Damien canonized (bottom photo).

Glossary

Aloha. The universal Hawaiian greeting, carrying meanings of kindness, warmth, and affection

Kanaka. Man, human being. The general nineteenth-century term for Hawaiians

Kanawai. Law. As in He Kanawai E Kaohi Ai I Ka Laha Ana O Ka Mai Lepera—An Act To Prevent The Spread of Leprosy

Kokua. To help, or a helper, used to describe Hawaiians who went voluntarily to the settlement at Kalawao to be with family members or friends

Lepera. Leprosy

Maikai. Good

Makua. Father

Pali. Cliff, precipice. The promontory of Kalawao is walled off from the rest of the island of Moloka'i by a thousand-foot pali

Poi. The Hawaiian staple food, made from cooked taro, pounded into a paste

Puhala. Pandanus tree. In Damien's first weeks at Kalawao, he sheltered under a puhala, and it became his chosen gravesite

Further Reading

Damien's letters to his family are collected in the archives of the Congregation of the Sacred Hearts in Louvain, Belgium. His letters to his superiors in the Hawaiʻi mission, and letters from Hawaiians at the settlement, are in the Sacred Hearts archives in Kāneʻohe, Hawaiʻi. His letters to the mother house of the Sacred Hearts are in the archives of the Congregation in Rome. His letters and reports from Kalawao to the Board of Health of the Hawaiian Kingdom are in the Hawaiʻi State Archives in Honolulu.

Volumes of official documentation assembled in connection with the beatification and canonization of Damien contain testimony by witnesses to his life at Kalawao, including by Hawaiians confined to the settlement. *Beatificationis et Canonizationis Servi Dei Damiani De Veuster, Missionarii, Sacerdotis Congregationis SS. Cordium de Picpus, Positio Super Cause Introductione* (Rome, Guerra e Belli, 1954), and *Beatificationis et Canonizationis Servi Dei Damiani De Veuster, Missionari, Sacerdotis Professi, Congregationis SS. Cordium Jesu et Mariae (Picpus), Positio Super Virtutibus* (Rome, Guerra e Belli, 1966).

For those interested in learning more about Damien, his work, his life and times, and his legacy, these books are useful—

Brocker, James H. *The Lands of Father Damien: Kalaupapa, Molokai, Hawaii.* Kalaupapa: James H. Brocker, 1998.

Bunson, Margaret R., and Matthew E. Bunson. *St. Damien of Molokai: Apostle of the Exiled.* Huntington, IN: Our Sunday Visitor, 2009.

Cahill, Emmett. *Yesterday at Kalaupapa: A Saga of Pain and Joy.* Honolulu: Editions Limited, Mutual Publishing, 1990.

Case, Howard D., ed. *Joseph Dutton, His Memoirs.* Honolulu: Star-Bulletin, 1931.

Clifford, Edward. *Father Damien: A Journey from Cashmere to His Home in Hawaii.* London: Macmillan, 1890.

Daws, Gavan. *Holy Man: Father Damien of Molokai.* New York: Harper & Row, 1973.

De Veuster, Pamphile. *Life and Letters of Father Damien, the Apostle of the Lepers.* London: Catholic Truth Society, 1889.

Dutton, Charles J. *The Samaritans of Molokai: The Lives of Father Damien and Brother Dutton Among the Lepers.* New York: Dodd, Mead, 1932.

Hanley, Mary Laurence and O. A. Bushnell. *A Song of Pilgrimage and Exile*. Honolulu: Mutual Publishing, 2009.

Jourdain, Vital. *The Heart of Father Damien*. Milwaukee: Bruce, 1955.

The King Kamehameha I and Father Damien Memorial Statues. Washington: U.S. Government Printing Office, 1970.

Law, Anwei Skinsnes and Henry G. Law. *Father Damien: A Bit of Taro, A Piece of Fish, and A Glass of Water*. Seneca Falls, New York: IDEA Center, 2009.

Levin, Wayne. *Kalaupapa: A Portrait*. Honolulu: Bishop Museum Press, 1989.

Mouritz, Arthur A. *"The Path of the Destroyer": A History of Leprosy in the Hawaiian Islands and Thirty Years of Research into the Means by Which It Has Been Spread*. Honolulu: Star-Bulletin Press, 1916.

Stevenson, Robert Louis. *Father Damien: An Open Letter to the Reverend Doctor Hyde of Honolulu*. Sydney: n.p., 1890.

Stoddard, Charles Warren. *Charles Warren Stoddard's Diary of a Visit to Molokai in 1884*. San Francisco: The Book Club of California, 1933.

Stoddard, Charles Warren. *The Lepers of Molokai*. Notre Dame: Ave Maria Press, 1893.

Tayman, John. *The Colony*. New York: Scribner, 2006.

Woods, G.W. *Reminiscences of a Visit, in July, 1876, to the Leper Settlement of Molokai, Having Special Reference to Rev. Father J. Damien Deveuster*. N.p., n.d.

Photo Credits

Associated Press: page 114

Hawaiian Historical Society: page 46

Hawaii Catholic Herald: pages 115, 116

Hawai'i State Archives: pages 4, 8, 10, 14, 17, 22, 29 (top), 30, 37, 45 48, 50, 53, 56, 61, 66, 72, 88 (top), 98, 99

Honolulu Advertiser: pages 100 (Kim Taylor Reece), 105, 110

Honolulu Star-Bulletin: pages xii (Dennis Oda), 27 (George F. Lee, top photos), 34 (Craig T. Kojima, top photos), 58 (George F. Lee), 85 (bottom photos), 94 (George F. Lee, top photo), 106

Mutual Publishing: page 84

Notre Dame University: page 70

Pan Pacific Press Bureau: page 6

Patrick Boland: page 38

Sacred Hearts Archives, Kāne'ohe: pages 7, 29 (bottom), 31, 33, 47

Sacred Hearts Archives, Louvain: pages xiv, 2, 3, 12, 26, 27 (bottom), 28, 32, 39, 41, 42, 43, 57, 60, 62, 78, 83, 85 (top), 88 (bottom), 90, 91, 93, 95, 96, 107, 108

ulukau.org: page 19

Wayne Levin: page 15

Wisconsin Historical Society: page 34 (inset)